# Making The Grade

How Boards Can Ensure Academic Quality

# Grade

## By Peter T. Ewell

Association of Governing Boards of Universities and Colleges

Development of this book was generously supported by the James S. Kemper Foundation

*Making the Grade:*
*How Boards Can Ensure Academic Quality*

Printed and bound in the United States of America.

Library of Congress Cataloging-in-Publication Data

Ewell, Peter.
Making the grade : how boards can ensure academic quality / by Peter T. Ewell.
    p. cm.
Includes bibliographical references and index.
    ISBN 0-9754948-6-4
    1. Universities and colleges—United States—Evaluation. 2. Universities and colleges—United States—Administration. 3. Quality assurance—United States. I. Title.
LB2331.63.E94 2006
378.1'01—dc22
2006033556

# Contents

# Foreword

Accountability has become the true watchword in higher education: The public, wondering whether colleges and universities are really as effective as they claim to be, demands evidence of high academic quality and achievement. What's more, there is a troubling gap between public perceptions of what constitutes academic quality and the complex realities facing institutions and their governing boards. Most often, accountability discussions center only on costs and financial measures to the relative detriment of less tangible but equally important issues surrounding the academic enterprise. Yet governing boards need better data to measure progress and better understanding of the real steps institutions should take in pursuit of academic excellence. This pursuit requires trustees and governing boards to be fully engaged and focused in discussing the critical issues surrounding academic quality.

Much "hard time" is spent by faculty, provosts, deans, and others at public and private institutions discussing the nature of teaching and learning. In fact, these discussions are among the most exciting conversations on campus. Boards need to take an active part in these exchanges—indeed, they should want very much to be an integral part of these discussions that essentially reach to the heart of the higher education enterprise. The board's need to inform itself about academic achievement should rank high on the scale of fiduciary responsibility, as the quality of the learning experience is a primary indicator of the effectiveness and reputation of the institution.

Framing questions to ask about academic quality is not a simple task. Trustees also must develop more than a superficial understanding of the issues behind the debate—in order to know what to do with the answers to their questions. In *Making the Grade: How Boards Can Ensure Academic Quality*, Peter Ewell—a foremost leader in the field of academic assessment, a widely published author, former faculty member, and a college trustee—has crafted a practical, persuasive guide that will help boards understand what is at stake in the accountability arena. The book strikes resounding chords of good sense, clear thinking, and thoughtful presentation and posits incisive questions about the academic enterprise. Ewell's perspective as a trustee, too, is evident in the book; he clarifies the inside-baseball discussions and opens them up for readers who may not know everything—or anything—about academic assessment and the tools that boards can use to scale their involvement with the issues related to teaching and learning.

Tightly focused and organized in six succinct chapters, each consisting of an "Overview" and the "Basics," followed by "Questions for Boards to Consider," the modest size of the book belies its sophistication and authoritative message. Ewell does no less than offer trustees a core of understanding that will help guide them to successful fulfillment of their oversight role in the academic areas. Each chapter forms a discrete inquiry into a component of the academic quality equation. The "Questions for Boards to Consider" section of each isn't just a laundry list of questions. Rather, Ewell frames the question and then presents varied ways boards can exercise their responsibilities in the balancing act of academic governance—an act Ewell believes can be achieved without shying away from the distinctions between appropriate board involvement and overreaching interference and without preempting faculty and other academic prerogatives.

AGB is grateful to the James S. Kemper Foundation (and extends a special thank-you to its former executive director, Thomas Hellie) for the generous grant that made this effort possible. *Making the Grade* crowns a multiyear, Kemper-funded project on the connection between governing boards and the academic enterprise of higher education. It builds naturally on and extends the discussions of *Strategic Leadership in Academic Affairs* by Richard L. Morrill, which AGB published in 2002. It also complements the other components issuing from under the grant's umbrella, including an AGB Board Basic, "The Board's Responsibilities for Academic Affairs," a national survey on academic affairs, and a series of significant discussions on the topic nationwide. *Making the Grade* provides yet more tools for boards to use in focusing on academic quality. AGB sincerely hopes this book signals the beginning of a trend in American higher education leading to more substantive and fruitful discussions among boards, faculty, and administrators about the most essential objective of any learning institution—ensuring academic quality.

**Susan Whealler Johnston**
*Executive Vice President*
*Association of Governing Boards*
*of Universities and Colleges*
*November 2006*

vi

*Foreword*

# Introduction

As board members, we are accustomed to looking after the financial health and fiscal integrity of our institutions. Virtually every board meeting we attend features reviews of budgets, revenue projections, capital needs, or the approval of specific expenditures. Many of us also sit on the foundation boards of our institutions, where examining specific investments and associated returns is the principal order of business. But at many institutions the board only rarely gets to look directly at the heart of the academic enterprise: the quality of teaching and learning.

There are many reasons why this is beginning to change. And change it should. As in the far-more-visible world of elementary and secondary education, the products of our colleges and universities are experiencing intensive public scrutiny because of the overwhelming importance of developing the nation's "educational capital" in a globally competitive world. At the same time, competition within higher education for more and better students means that attention to academic quality must be paramount if the institutions for which we are responsible are to prosper.

As in other realms of institutional operations, it is up to the faculty and administration to uphold and improve academic quality. But it is up to the board to understand it and to see that it gets done. Ensuring academic quality is a fiduciary responsibility; it is as much part of our role as board members as ensuring that the institution has sufficient resources and is spending them wisely.

Most boards have academic affairs committees that are responsible for broad oversight of the institution's academic functions, including programs, curricula, teaching, research, and faculty affairs. These committees have a specific responsibility for ensuring that academic quality assurance and improvement mechanisms are in place. They can be expected, for example, to look carefully at the evidence about student learning or the results of academic program review and engage in interpretive dialogue with senior academic administrators and faculty committee chairs to determine potential implications and what improvements can be made. Occasionally, such dialogue will result in a recommendation to the full board about a potential strategic direction with respect to academic programming or a needed investment. For small boards that have no discrete academic affairs committee, the full board will have to judiciously assume these responsibilities.

My intent in this book is to review the substance of what board members should know about the various dimensions of academic quality, the mechanisms colleges and universities use to investigate and improve it, and the kinds of questions we should ask our presidents and chief academic officers about how the institution is doing. I briefly examine the various changes that have occurred in both the academy and its operating context that now compel attention in ensuring academic quality. I then go on to review four major areas of academic quality assurance and improvement that boards should know about: (1) the assessment of student learning, (2) student retention and graduation, (3) stakeholder satisfaction, and (4) academic program review. Each of these is briefly described in terms of how the process works and the kinds of questions board members should ask about results. For each, moreover, I list responsibilities particularly appropriate to the academic affairs committee. A final chapter addresses institutional and program accreditation—the increasingly important process of external review that draws upon this internal evidence and certifies quality for the institution's many stakeholders.

## Defining the Territory.

One way to organize the processes that make up academic quality assurance and explain how they fit together is to visualize the institution's teaching and learning functions as they would work in a typical business enterprise. Given this perspective, questions such as the following will be familiar to most boards of directors in other settings:

- ***How good is our product?*** For colleges and universities, the principal product is student learning, and the quality of learning outcomes should be a central concern. And just as in a manufacturing enterprise, quality needs to be examined from at least two perspectives: the ultimate quality of the product on completion (what a student knows and can do upon graduation) and the "value added" by the "production process" of instruction (how much *more* a student knows and can do upon graduation than he or she did upon entering the institution). Determining these is the business of *assessment*.

- ***How good are we at producing our product?*** Like every other "production process," college-level instruction entails a certain amount of "waste." Not all who enter our institutions as freshmen will complete their programs, and many of those who do will "stop out" for some period of time or will otherwise finish late. Patterns of student flow into and through our institutions are important to monitor because they affect both costs and outcomes. As a result, every institution should know something about *student retention and graduation*.

- **Are our customers satisfied?** Like all businesses, colleges and universities have a range of stakeholders, and the perceptions they maintain about the institution are important to monitor because they will strongly affect whether the stakeholders continue to relate to and invest in us. Among the key stakeholders from whom we must seek such information are students, potential students and their parents, employers, civic opinion leaders, and members of the public in the regions we serve. Periodically examining *stakeholder perceptions and opinions* can help tailor our product and anticipate emerging needs.

- **Do we have the right "mix" of products?** Like businesses that typically offer diverse "product mixes," colleges and universities offer degrees in many fields and provide instruction at multiple levels. Regardless of the levels of outcomes achieved and the efficiency of the production process, therefore, institutions should periodically take stock of their "product portfolios" to determine whether they are offering the right things at the right levels in the light of graduate quality and the marketplace. Stock-taking of this kind is typically a part of *academic program review*.

- **Do we make the grade?** Finally, businesses that want to stay competitive must obtain external certifications or ratings of their quality. For products, this may take the form of earning certification by Underwriter's Laboratory or obtaining the Good Housekeeping Seal of Approval. Companies themselves can pursue international quality certifications such as ISO9001 or seek the Malcolm Baldrige National Quality Award. For colleges and universities, this basic quality certification is *institutional accreditation*, and it is critical for institutions if they are to remain in good standing.

    Analogies between the academy and the world of business, of course, can be overdrawn. But characterizing some of the basic processes of academic management and quality assurance in business language emphasizes the fact that academic affairs should not be considered alien territory by members of the board who do not happen to be academics. Familiar principles of wise management and judicious oversight should inform these functions just as they do any other.

# Defining the Board's Role.

The basic questions posed here are not only colloquial but are intentionally pitched at a level appropriate for board involvement. The role of the board in academic quality assurance, as in any other area, needs to be defined in terms of explicit boundary conditions that guard against overstepping the line between necessary fiduciary responsibility for the institution and directly managing its operations. This is always a delicate balance, and it is more so in academic affairs where issues tend to be more complex and lines of authority less clear-cut than in more "businesslike" areas of institutional functioning such as finance, personnel management, communications, and fund-raising.

Issues are more complex in part because faculty from different disciplines may have different values with respect to what is most important in the curriculum and what constitutes "high quality" performance. There is a lot more ambiguity in these matters than in whether the fiscal bottom line is black or red. Lines of authority are less clear-cut because academic matters typically are managed by consensus, and individual faculty and departments are legitimately accorded a great deal of autonomy in defining what they do with respect to instruction and in carrying it out. Both of these factors mean that coming to closure on academic matters may take a good deal of time.

On the one hand, this means that boards need to display patience in allowing the process of academic deliberation to run its course. On the other, board members need to continue to press for answers and avoid the temptation to stop asking questions just because the process seems stalled.

For boards that have an academic affairs committee, these dialogues become deeper, and the need to maintain appropriate balance becomes even more important. Academic affairs committees, for example, will be expected to examine evidence of academic quality in greater detail than the full board and discuss emerging implications with academic leaders and senior faculty members. These discussions may well raise questions about curricular change, the need for greater attention to faculty development, potentially significant investments in instructional technology, or program inventory. Because of their unique position of being able to see such evidence from the point of view of the institution as a whole, rather than from the perspective of particular departments or schools, committee members may be able to shed a different interpretive light on some of this evidence and should not hesitate to do so. But as for the board as a whole, committee members should be mindful that their role is about strategic direction, not the details of how things should be done.

One way to begin to achieve clarity with respect to the board's proper role in these matters is to consider the following principles:

- ***Running the curriculum is the faculty's responsibility; the board's role is to remind them of that responsibility.*** Principles of shared governance at any institution mean that primary responsibility for the academic program is vested in its faculty. This means that faculty first must define the learning outcomes students are expected to achieve in each academic program and for the institution as a whole and then design and deliver a curriculum consistent with these objectives. *This is a collective responsibility.* Although it is normal for there to be a good deal of variance with respect to how each faculty member teaches toward established learning objectives, it is both appropriate and important for the board to insist that all faculty *have* such objectives, that instructors are conscious about designing learning activities consistent with these objectives, and that they are collecting evidence that these objectives are being attained.

What is important for the board is to remind the faculty that these expectations are an integral part of their academic responsibility. It is beyond the board's appropriate role to question or dictate the *content* of these intended outcomes or the particular instructional designs and approaches used to achieve them.

- **Stay focused on strategic issues.** Strategic issues are "mission-critical"—that is, they are issues that if left unattended will threaten the institution's ability to fulfill its purposes. Balanced budgets are mission-critical, which is why boards pay so much attention to achieving them. All of the "basic business questions" noted earlier are mission-critical in this sense. For example, student retention is mission-critical because it affects both tuition revenue and the reputation the institution needs to attract new students. Similarly, program mix is mission-critical because it both defines the student markets the institution tries to tap and because it delineates the boundaries of the type of institution it aspires to be. Above all, maintaining the quality of student-learning outcomes is mission-critical because it validates the claims the institution is making about its graduates—claims that if unsubstantiated will affect graduates' employment and postgraduate opportunities and ultimately the institution's ability to attract new students.

  In this regard, strategic questions reflect how well the institution is doing its basic job of graduating students who are competent and well prepared. They should not address the specific changes needed in response to negative assessment results. Similarly, strategic questions reflect the new opportunities for institutional markets or programs that may be revealed in the course of a program review. They are not about designing the content or instructional approaches that will characterize new programs.

- **Expect and demand a culture of evidence.** In the past, colleges and universities viewed academic quality as an intangible—impossible to measure and in the eye of the beholder. This traditional view rested largely on institutional resources and reputation as a proxy for academic quality. The current premise of academic quality assurance is entirely the opposite—that it is possible to assemble meaningful and generalizable evidence of academic quality and to act on it to improve teaching and learning. But because many of these processes are new and unfamiliar, there remains a tendency at many institutions to make assertions about student learning or program quality based largely on anecdote.

  Boards should not let that happen. Conversations about academic quality in any of its dimensions should be based on *evidence*. Boards should insist on this, and administrators and faculty members should come to expect it. Whenever claims about quality, effectiveness, or improvement are made, boards should always ask, "How do we know that?" If evidence-based answers are not offered, the follow-up question should be "What would it take to find out?"

Under many circumstances, adequate evidence may not be available for legitimate reasons. Methodologies for gathering appropriate evidence in some areas may be unavailable, inapplicable to the institution's circumstances, or simply too expensive to pursue cost effectively. But the board nevertheless has a responsibility to ask the questions.

- ***Recognize that evidence about academic quality raises issues but rarely gives final answers.*** Much of the evidence generated by academic quality reviews ends up being presented in numeric form and, as a result, has an air of precision that suggests "final answers." In fact, on most occasions these data will represent not the end but the beginning of a conversation. This will be the case particularly in the deliberations of the academic affairs committee, where evidence about academic quality should be regularly presented and thoroughly discussed. When presented with such data, committee members should not just take them at face value but should ask administrators what *they* think the data mean and what action implications grow out of the findings.

  In looking at information like this, moreover, committee members should be aware that such statistics mean little without an interpretive context. One way of providing context is to establish a point of comparison. For example, committee members might ask how a given statistic about academic performance compares with the same information from the previous year or to similar figures nationally or for a set of peer institutions. Another way to provide context is by breaking down the statistic further to examine how it looks for different campus populations. For example, questions might be raised about how men performed in comparison with women, how particular academic programs fared in comparison with one another, or how students receiving institutional aid performed.

  Further, because academic quality is complex and elusive, no single piece of evidence tells the whole story. Committee members instead should ask administrators to provide evidence drawn from multiple sources and to engage the campus in holistic conversation about the "big picture" that emerges from a presented body of evidence.

- ***Make reviewing evidence of academic quality and improvement a regular and expected board-level activity.*** It is easy in the context of pressing board business such as approving budgets, looking at construction progress reports, and handling legal matters to put off looking at academics. Yet teaching and learning constitutes every institution's main business, and academic quality should be of paramount concern to the board. Because the faculty and administration bear most of this responsibility, the board's overall level of engagement in this area need not be time-consuming—but it does need to be systematic. This implies that regular occasions to consider information about academic quality should be built into the board's annual schedule. This can be done in many ways, including annual reviews by the full board of "dashboard" performance indicators that contain data on academic quality, making discussions of quality an integral part of a strategic planning exercise, or making assessment results a topic for a board retreat where more in-depth conversations can occur.

Reviewing results of each of the four sources of evidence about academic quality (discussed in detail in subsequent chapters) should be an explicit responsibility of the academic affairs committee, which should establish a regular schedule for doing so in collaboration with academic leadership. Finally, the full board should be aware of preparations for institutional accreditation—a process that today focuses more heavily on the assessment of student-learning outcomes—and should thoroughly discuss the resulting accreditation report with administrators to determine what should be done in response.

The overall message here is that knowledge about the academic condition of the enterprise is as critical for a board as knowledge about the institution's fiscal condition. As Harvard University's Derek Bok put it in a 2005 essay in the *Chronicle of Higher Education*: "The traditional roles of trustees are *both* to defend and promote the interests of their institutions *and* to represent the concerns and needs of the public that does much to subsidize and sustain higher education. Examining the methods used to ensure the quality of education is a natural way of discharging the second role."

Yet it is important to keep the board's involvement *strategic* by ensuring (1) that the right kinds of academic quality-assurance processes are in place and (2) by periodically asking questions about how the administration is using the information it collects about the academic effectiveness to improve teaching and learning.

To reiterate, the board has a fiduciary responsibility to ensure that the institution is meeting its obligations. In this regard, a favorable accreditation outcome is as important to an institution as a clean financial audit. The board also must be assured that the administration is effectively managing the institution and is using tools and approaches consistent with known best practices in academic management. Among these practices are learning assessment, monitoring student flow, seeking feedback from students and stakeholders, and regularly reviewing the quality of academic programs.

The board as a whole, or through its academic affairs committee, ensures that these important processes are in place and are functioning effectively by requiring reports by the president and chief academic officer on their results and on the issues of academic quality that the results raise each year. It is as important for the board to know that these mechanisms are in place and that their results are being used as it is for the board to know that the institution is following sound budgeting and accounting practices.

Finally, as in any corporation, the board has ultimate responsibility for the soundness of the institution's products and the integrity of its operations. At bottom, this means that it must be able to stand behind the competitiveness of the institution's graduates with respect to their knowledge and skills and the academic integrity of the curriculum that prepared them. This is what we signify when we stand with our faculty and graduates at every commencement convocation. We need to act on this testimony in the boardroom.

# CHAPTER 1

# The New Interest in Academic Quality

For many years, the substance of "quality" in higher education lay almost solely in the domains of reputation, inputs, and productivity. Publicly funded institutions, for example, routinely reported on the preparation levels of students they admitted and unit costs in relation to enrollments and student credit hours. Regional accreditors, charged with examining the adequacy of public and private institutions alike, looked mostly at the overall level of institutional resources and at internal shared governance processes. Where each of these reporting processes touched the realm of academic affairs, it was largely to examine curricular structures and faculty credentials.

Over the past two decades, however, interest on the part of external stakeholders in the actual academic performance of colleges and universities steadily has risen. There are a number of reasons for this. One is a growing atmosphere of accountability in higher education, with an emphasis on student learning outcomes. Another is increased competitiveness in the higher education marketplace, an environment that puts a premium on visible evidence of academic performance. A third stimulus is the constrained fiscal conditions under which most colleges and universities operate today—a context that puts a premium on sound and evidence-based academic management practices as much as it does on fiscal discipline.

## Accountability.

Beginning in the mid-1980s, state policymakers grew concerned about the outcomes of higher education in relation to its costs. Educational quality already was on the minds of governors and state legislators because of the "A Nation at Risk" report in 1983, which warned of declining learning standards in elementary and secondary schools. In this climate, the National Governors Association launched an initiative titled "Time for Results," extending a call to examine the quality of collegiate learning that continues to reverberate. One result has been the birth of a nation-wide "assessment movement" in higher education that has stimulated the development of systematic investigations of student-learning outcomes at

1

*Making The Grade*

growing numbers of colleges and universities. Another has been significant new attention to graduation rates in higher education—a topic not much attended to before this point.

The explicit interest of states in higher education quality embraces more than just public institutions and is driven by three factors. First, state governments are "owner-operators" of public colleges and universities, which they directly fund and oversee. As such, state policymakers are fundamentally interested in cost-effectiveness and return on investment. With respect to outcomes, this means that policymakers want to be assured that graduates have reached acceptable levels of academic performance in relation to costs. But they also are concerned about such matters as student retention and the time it takes students to earn their degrees because these are assumed to be related to efficiency as well.

Second, many states provide substantial scholarship support that allows students to attend private as well as public institutions. Acting in this role, a state's primary concern with respect to academic quality assurance is that students obtain a credential of value—one with which graduates are satisfied and that has a payoff in the marketplace for employment.

Finally, in their roles as "keepers of the public interest," states are concerned about such things as economic development, civic participation, and overall quality of life for their citizens. Dimensions of quality in higher education that interest them in this regard include college and university contributions to economic development in the form of well-prepared graduates, contributions to knowledge consistent with state need, and institutional responsiveness to regional and community needs. These elements of quality, of course, can be manifest in both public and private institutions.

While these basic interests in academic accountability are common across the 50 states, they differ in the ways in which they emerge. A few states require students at public institutions to pass standardized examinations and/or participate in statewide surveys about what they experienced and what they learned. Far more states require public institutions to report regularly on student outcomes using institution-defined criteria and assessment methods. Finally, almost every state includes graduation rates as part of its performance-indicator system for public higher education, and some states are beginning to include private institutions in these reports as well. Some of these states have data on student progress at independent colleges collected by virtue of these institutions' participation in state-funded student-aid programs.

Increasingly, though, institutional accrediting organizations are displacing states as the primary actor in quality assurance for higher education. Accreditation is a nominally voluntary process that began about a century ago as a means for colleges and universities to recognize and accept one another's credits and credentials. To remain accredited, institutions go through a comprehensive review process at least once every ten years that involves preparation of a self-study, one or more multi-day visits by a team of peer reviewers, and a review report noting institutional strengths and areas for improvement together with a judgment regarding the institution's continuing accreditation status. (See Chapter 6 for details.)

The "teeth" in accreditation lies in the fact that institutions must remain accredited to continue to participate in the U.S. Education Department's extensive financial-aid programs, which include both need-based aid and low-interest student loans. Most colleges and universities participate heavily in these programs, which provide them a significant component of tuition revenue.

The link between accreditation and federal funds exists because the federal government essentially has "deputized" accrediting organizations to review institutional quality on its behalf, in lieu of creating an extensive and expensive federal accountability process for higher education. In order to ensure that they are doing what the federal government wants, accrediting organizations are themselves periodically reviewed by the Education Department and officially "recognized" as gatekeepers for federal funds. And since about 1990, one of the most prominent conditions for continuing recognition is a requirement that accrediting organizations emphasize the assessment of student learning in their reviews of institutions. The result has been a significant increase in the salience with which this matter is treated when accrediting teams visit campuses. This is one of the most important reasons why board members should be aware of their institution's activities in assessing student learning outcomes and about how faculty and staff are using assessment results to improve teaching and learning.

Although accountability demands on colleges and universities have increased markedly over the past decade, there is mounting evidence that these demands will only increase. The 2004-05 academic year was especially notable in signaling this direction. At the beginning of that year, a report by the Business Higher Education Forum (BHEF)—a prominent national advocacy group for employers—published a report on accountability that called on all institutions to provide public evidence about their graduates' levels of learning. Next, the State Higher Education Executive Officers (SHEEO) convened a National Commission on Accountability, which called on states to periodically assess "educational capital" in the form of benchmarked measures of student learning. Its report reinforced the BHEF's message that all institutions need to assess the student-learning outcomes of its graduates and report results to the public. Finally, the Association of American Colleges and Universities (AACU) issued a report urging institutions to move aggressively toward assessing student-learning outcomes common to all degrees.

These three reports are harbingers of an institutional operating environment in which accountability for academic quality will play an increasingly larger part. Board members need to know about the growing salience of accountability as a driver of demands for evidence of academic quality and to ensure that their institutions are in a position to respond.

# Competitiveness.

For most public institutions, state funding has become a steadily diminishing share of revenues. These institutions must make up for the shortfalls by raising tuition, a tactic most private institutions have depended on to sustain their revenues. This means that maintaining enrollment is a critical concern for all colleges and universities today. But most institutions are not interested in simply "maintaining enrollment." Instead, they want to recruit and attract a specific kind of student body. This has fostered an increasingly competitive environment, as growing numbers of public and private institutions try to attract the best (or most suitable) students available in their recruitment pools. Indeed, for many institutions, the traditional distinctions between public and private have disappeared. Both tend to recruit from the same markets, and both increasingly use mechanisms such as institutional aid to shape their enrollments.

Operating in this environment increasingly requires an understanding of academic quality, and evidence of quality can be a significant tool in enhancing the institution's competitiveness. Perhaps most emblematic of this phenomenon is the current dominance of the rankings published each fall by *U.S. News & World Report*, in a feature titled "America's Best Colleges." These rankings have been issued for more than two decades and are firmly established in the higher education landscape. But the actual role of the rankings—and perhaps more importantly, our attitudes toward them—are contradictory. The evidence is slim that the *U.S. News* rankings actually influence student choice very much, yet their symbolic value has become enormous.

Institutional leaders rightly want to maintain their standing in these rankings, even as they criticize the way the rankings are constructed and decry them as an invalid measure of quality. Board members need to understand this, and they should not become upset if the institution slips a few notches in the rankings. But they also need to understand that some of the statistical ingredients of the rankings—and some alternatives to them—*do* warrant monitoring to help shape the institution's enrollment-management strategies.

One of these components is the quality of entering students—a characteristic captured to some extent by the *U.S. News* rankings in the form of the percentage of applicants admitted. This statistic is flawed as a management indicator because many institutions have a limited pool of potential candidates that are attracted to them for their distinctive characteristics. These institutions tend to select a high proportion of applicants from this limited group, which usually includes adequate numbers of superior students. In addition to examining information on the size and shape of the admissions pool and the percentage and number of applicants admitted, the board should be aware of the admissions "yield"—the percentage admitted who actually enroll. Similarly, if the institution is fairly selective, it also will be important to look at the quality of the incoming class in terms of such standard indicators as high school class rank, SAT or ACT scores, and any special characteristics that students may exhibit. It should be noted that the *U.S. News* rankings no longer include data on yield.

A second important dimension of performance captured in part by the *U.S. News* rankings is the rate at which students complete their degrees. Graduation-rate reporting is a prominent element of accountability, and the federal government since 1989 has required all institutions to calculate these data using a standard methodology and to make these statistics available to potential students and their parents. But information of this sort also is important in strategic enrollment planning and recruitment. Board members first need to understand that graduation rates correlate highly with the academic ability of an incoming class and that increased selectivity almost always will result in increased retention. But boards also need to understand that "beating the odds" with respect to retaining students of middling ability is a more efficient way to maintain enrollments (and therefore revenue) than simply admitting more new freshmen who then drop out. These financial entailments of recruitment and retention are not always apparent, though they are important institutional strategies.

But the *U.S. News* rankings are rightly criticized for capturing few authentic dimensions of academic quality. In fact, recent research has demonstrated that overall, they have almost no relationship to the kinds of high-quality academic experiences associated with substantial learning gain. This has led to a number of efforts to develop alternative measures of institutional quality that focus to a greater extent on such experiences. The National Survey of Student Engagement (NSSE) was developed in the late 1990s for exactly this purpose. Questions on the survey ask students to report on their own behaviors, as well as on teaching and learning practices and other aspects of the institution's instructional environment that empirical research has shown to be significantly related to learning. In some notable cases, institutions using NSSE have posted their results as part of their marketing efforts—as a supplement or an alternative to the *U.S. News* rankings. Board members should be aware that alternative views of institutional quality exist and might better characterize the institution's mission and the educational setting it is trying to market.

# Evidence-Based Management.

A final factor fueling the focus on academic quality is the rise of new approaches to managing the curriculum and the teaching and learning processes. These approaches also have been stimulated in part by increased competitiveness. Institutions have found that better management of academic resources can help it achieve more on a fixed-resource base without sacrificing quality. Institutions originally developed some of the information tools behind these new approaches to generate statistics needed to respond to growing accountability demands. But much of the power of these approaches came from a different source: evidence-based management techniques such as Total Quality Management (TQM) and Continuous Quality Improvement (CQI), which emerged in business and manufacturing in the 1990s. Many board members drawn from the business and professional community are familiar with these techniques and, more important, the principles of evidence-based management that lie behind them. Where appropriate, these board members should ask administrators if and how they apply these principles.

Colleges and universities first began adopting quality-management techniques drawn from business to the functions in which these appeared to fit best—operations and maintenance of the physical plant, personnel management, financial services, and procurement, for example. Among the most commonly used techniques were "mapping" standardized processes (such as cutting a reimbursement check) for the purpose of streamlining them, statistical process control (in such areas as purchasing) to ensure reliable consistent service, and outsourcing such functions as food services and computing. More recently, however, some of these same techniques have been fruitfully applied to processes related to teaching and learning.

These applications all center on achieving a better understanding of the academic "production function"—that is, how students flow through a set of courses in a particular curriculum, what they experience, and the outcomes they achieve. Particular attention usually is paid here to how particular sequences of courses "fit together" so that students are immediately able to apply what they have learned in the appropriate settings. The effectiveness of these connections can be monitored by looking at how students perform in subsequent courses in a sequence in relation to what they experienced and how they performed in previous (prerequisite) courses in the same sequence.

These techniques have proved to be especially applicable in fields such as mathematics and in remedial coursework in which it is possible to specify and teach to concrete learning outcomes, enabling much more effective and coherent learning experiences to be established. They also have proved especially important in the growing arena of technology-mediated instructional delivery.

Colleges and universities also are using the principles of evidence-based management to make decisions about the overall shape of the institution's academic offerings: what kinds of programs to offer in what fields and at what levels. Increasingly, these decisions are based in part on careful market research and needs analysis to determine the nature and extent of demand and to establish pricing policies. At the same time, current patterns of enrollment, retention and completion, assessment results, and job or graduate-school placement data are systematically examined to help determine whether the institution's current array of programs is optimal. This, in turn, may lead to evidence-based decisions about whether to expand capacity in a given program, scale it back, or eliminate the program altogether. These are, of course, the kinds of decisions that academic administrators have always had to make. The difference is that the decisions increasingly are based on concrete evidence, using a growing array of indicators of program need and performance.

- It is important for board members to recognize, of course, that there are limits on the applicability of quality-management techniques in academic settings. Teaching and learning are not the same as making widgets. Just because board members are familiar with such applications in other settings does not mean that they can commend them to academic leaders without qualification. But it is equally important for academic leaders to become aware of the appropriate potential applications, and the board's questions may be a good stimulus.

- These three conditions of doing business in the new academy—escalating accountability demands, increased competitiveness in the market for students, and the development of evidence-based management techniques to help deal with fiscal realities—together point to a growing need for new kinds of information about academic quality. Board members should realize that these conditions are not going to recede anytime soon and have quickly become permanent features of the higher education landscape. These forces are shaping institutional behavior in important ways. Consequently, boards need to advocate for having the right kinds of evidence-gathering and quality-management systems in place in the realm of teaching and learning as much as they now advocate for new sources of revenues and greater operating efficiencies in the institution's nonacademic functions.

To put it succinctly, under this new reality, colleges and universities can no more do without a systematic program of student outcomes assessment than they could do without a development office.

# CHAPTER 2

# Assessing Student-Learning Outcomes

**M**any board members may be surprised to learn that systematic investigations of what students know and can do as a result of attending a college or university have emerged only in the past 20 years at most American institutions. Unlike our counterparts in the United Kingdom and elsewhere in the English-speaking world, U.S. institutions do not employ "external examiners" to provide an outside check on student academic performance. Nor do we have national subject examinations as do many European countries such as France and Germany.

Instead, the historic U.S. approach to delivering an undergraduate curriculum gives individual faculty members the authority to run their courses as they see fit, awarding familiar letter grades to certify student performance. Passing the requisite numbers, types, and levels of courses in this manner in most cases fulfills the requirements for a baccalaureate degree—though many institutions now require "capstone" courses, or exercises at the end of a student's program. All that is typically known about a typical student's *overall* performance in college, then, is how many credits she or he completed, as well as a grade-point average calculated on the basis of grades awarded by 40-50 individual faculty members.

As long as few questions were asked about the quality of graduates' overall learning, this approach seemed acceptable. But when such questions began to surface in the early 1980s, grades alone no longer sufficed. Because it is common for the topic of grades to come up during discussions of how to assess student-learning outcomes, board members ought to know why this is the case and how the arguments unfold.

First, even if one assumes that faculty-awarded grades are valid and consistent, these grades address only the domain of a particular class and its specific content. Further, because an instructor may take a student's generic abilities such as writing into account when awarding grades, there is no way to know how much weight any two faculty members assign to such abilities in the grading process.

Second, even if it is clear exactly what all faculty are assessing when they grade, and the weight they give to each sub-ability, there is no assurance of consistency across the standards they use when they award, say, a B. In addition, grades generally are "normed" across the class population, with a given proportion of students expected for each possible grade. But this may

9

*Making The Grade*

mean that almost nobody in the class actually came up to the faculty member's previously established standard. Perhaps most important, the distribution of grades awarded in a given class indicates nothing about the patterns of strengths and weaknesses of the class *as a whole* with respect to learning—information that, if available, could be used to make improvements.

Assessment of student learning arose as an imperative for higher education when the answers to these kinds of questions began to become important—either for reasons of accountability or for reasons of academic improvement.

# The Basics.

Academic assessment comprises a set of systematic methods for collecting valid and reliable evidence of what students know and can do at various stages in their academic careers. "Know" implies the familiar cognitive dimension of learned concepts or disciplinary content—for example, a biological taxonomy, the principles of accounting, or the writings of the major Victorian poets. "Can do" implies the performance dimension of learning most frequently manifested in the form of a demonstrable skill—for example, the ability to write a succinct paragraph that critiques an argument, to design and carry out a physics experiment, or to debug a computer program.

Occasionally, "affective" or "attitudinal" dimensions are added to this list—for example, tolerance for diversity and the ability to operate in a diverse or global environment, ethical behavior, or a sense of personal responsibility. Assessment may mean gathering evidence about any of these attributes. It can be undertaken at the discipline or major program level, for the institution's general education program, or for the institution as a whole—and most institutions will conduct all three kinds of assessments.

Any assessment is governed by formal statements of "intended learning outcomes" that are developed by a program's faculty or for the institution as a whole. For employment-related programs or for programs with specialized accreditation, these statements frequently are developed in consultation with employers or professional associations. For more traditional academic disciplines such as psychology and political science, national disciplinary associations increasingly are developing "model" sets of program-level student-learning outcomes that faculty can use as guides.

To establish statements of more general student-learning outcomes—those expected of all of the institution's graduates, for example—a frequent starting point is the mission statement, which generally says something about the qualities the institution seeks to instill in its graduates. But the language contained in most mission statements illustrates the challenge associated with constructing meaningful statements of intended learning outcomes: It is so vague and general that it provides little guidance for gathering evidence. Adequate learning-outcomes statements, in contrast, are cast in active language ("graduates safely handle chemical materials taking into account their physical and chemical properties, including any specific hazards associated with their use") and are sufficiently concrete to enable an actual task or demonstration to be constructed ("graduates can summarize and explain the findings of an empirical study in sociology, including a critical assessment of the methodological frameworks used").

Finally, academic assessment programs are designed primarily to collect information about student performance in the *aggregate* in order to ground judgments about overall program quality or to uncover general strengths and weaknesses that can be used as the basis for further program development. Their primary purpose is to draw general conclusions about teaching and learning, not about individual people. This makes them different from certification programs that govern entry into a profession—for example, state bar exams or medical licensing procedures. Evidence from licensure or certification may be used in institutional assessment, but the intent is to analyze and disaggregate this evidence to learn something about how the *program* is functioning, not just to count the number of individuals who passed. The fact that the unit of analysis is collective instead of individual also means that the evaluator need not assess all students. In many cases, samples of student work or performance are used because this may be adequate to draw valid conclusions.

Because many board members may be more familiar with the assessment procedures currently used in elementary and secondary education than with those in collegiate settings, a few words about the differences are in order. Under the federal No Child Left Behind law, all elementary schoolchildren in certain grades must be tested using standardized achievement examinations developed by each state. Performance on these examinations is used to compare schools, and low-performing schools are sanctioned as a result. Although much criticized, these procedures are in part justifiable because all schoolchildren are supposed to learn the same things at the same levels regardless of where they go to school. Furthermore, the knowledge and skills in question are relatively easy to test.

Higher education differs from this more familiar school context in at least two ways. First, colleges differ widely with respect to mission, so it is legitimate to expect differences in the learning outcomes they seek to foster in their students. As a result, institution-based efforts to assess student-learning outcomes vary from place to place with respect both to the outcomes institutions examine and the kinds of evidence they use in the process. Second, at the collegiate level, higher order learning outcomes are complex and therefore difficult to measure. As a result, though standardized test results sometimes are used, so is a wide range of other evidence, including essays, specially designed assignments, projects, demonstrations, and portfolios. There is a good deal of appropriate variety across colleges and universities with respect to the shape of their assessment programs, and boards should not expect much standardization. What they *should* ensure is that the methods used and the outcomes assessed are consistent with the institution's mission and values.

# Questions for Boards to Consider.

Because assessment is so deeply rooted in and driven by the curriculum, it is chiefly a faculty concern. Faculty need to fully own the learning outcomes used to drive the assessment process and should be the primary actors involved in developing them. But the board should become broadly familiar with the basic features of the academic assessment program and ask judicious questions about it. Members of the academic affairs committee should expect to see and discuss assessment results with academic leaders and faculty committee chairs on a regular basis. Among the most important questions boards can ask about assessment are the following:

1. ***Do we say what and how much students should learn? Where do we say it?*** Institutions that seek to earn accreditation today are required to develop and state formal learning-outcomes statements for each of academic program (or department) as well as for general education (or the degree as a whole). Yet it is surprising how many institutions are not yet in compliance with this requirement, especially at the program level. Boards should therefore assure themselves that their institution meets this most basic requirement and should act aggressively to direct the institution's leadership to address the situation promptly if it does not. Moreover, statements of learning outcomes not only should describe the ability in question, they also should provide some guidance about the *level* at which the ability will be demonstrated. Many of the statements currently in place could be improved in this respect because they provide little guidance—either in their configuration or in the kinds of assessment evidence that they require—about how good is "good enough."

   More important than merely being present in the institution's publications, statements of intended learning outcomes should be familiar to faculty. Too often, such statements are developed by only a few individuals acting largely to ensure that the institution meets basic accreditation requirements, but they have not become part of the academic fabric of the institution—internalized by faculty as collective goals for teaching and used systematically to inform instructional development and grading. In contrast, accrediting organizations increasingly are looking for deeper "cultures of evidence," in which goals for learning are widely shared and discussed among faculty, and they are getting steadily better at determining whether such cultures are present. Some are using techniques such as the European "academic audit," in which two or three academic departments are selected at random for a "drill down" review to see how processes such as assessment actually work on the ground. Boards should ask academic administrators about the institution's current status in this regard. If they were to be "audited" today, what proportion of departments and faculty would report appropriately?

Because they are intended to be used as guides for curriculum development and to establish standards against which to judge learning, statements of intended learning outcomes also should be accessible to students in catalogues, course descriptions, and syllabi. The latter are perhaps most important because students will learn best when they are aware of the concrete expectations in terms of which their performances on tests and assignments will be judged. Including learning outcomes in syllabi also provides an opportunity for faculty to let students know *why* they are being asked to do certain things in a given class or learning experience. Too often, students see course requirements only as requirements—set arbitrarily by faculty without much connection to an overarching goal. Helping them perceive a clear path of development and the reasons why certain things are being asked of them can help students overcome the all-too-typical lack of motivation to perform that many exhibit when they believe learning activities or assignments are irrelevant to their own situations or goals.

Finally, statements of intended learning outcomes can help focus and differentiate the institution's marketing and student-recruitment efforts. Every institution tries to be distinctive in the message it sends to potential students, stakeholders, and donors. Among the most powerful areas of distinction are the claims it makes for its graduates. The more precise and compelling the institution can render these descriptors—and the more persuasive it can be in deploying evidence of their achievement—the more advantage it will have in the marketplace. This will be especially true in the future as employers and graduate programs increasingly seek concrete evidence of student achievement beyond grade-point averages.

In all these areas, boards should assure themselves that learning-outcomes statements are in place and visible. At least as important, they should ask whether the goals established are consistent with the institution's mission. Do they communicate the distinctive abilities and values for which the institution stands? These questions do not abrogate faculty prerogative. Instead, they lie at the heart of the board's important role of ensuring the institution's basic purposes.

2. ***What kinds of evidence do we collect about learning?*** Boards, and especially the members of the academic affairs committees, also need to be broadly familiar with the kinds of assessment processes being used at the institution to gather or assemble evidence that learning outcomes are being achieved. This is most straightforwardly accomplished by a regular look at the institution's assessment plan or schedule, often developed in concert with an established system of program review. A plan of this kind is one of the first things that a visiting accreditation team will want to see, and they may want to "drill down" to the level of individual programs and interview faculty mem-

bers to see if the plan is real. In this context, it is especially important for board members to ask the administration to review the established assessment plan well in advance of an accreditation visit and to provide the board with an honest appraisal of overall progress as well as plans to address any difficulties.

Academic affairs committees, in turn, should be expected to know a bit more detail about how such evidence is collected and used to improve teaching and learning. In reviewing the actual contents of the assessment plan, committee members should recognize that there are many appropriate ways to gather evidence about student achievement and that faculty members are best suited to determine what these might be. Committee members need to be aware of some important distinctions among different kinds of assessment-based evidence.

First, assessments usually are distinguished as *direct* or *indirect*. Direct assessment methods such as examinations, assignments, and tasks demand that the ability in question be observed palpably and immediately. Indirect assessment, in contrast, uses methods that do not examine learning itself but rather its consequences—related behaviors such as job placements and civic participation or self-reports about learning gains as reported through questionnaires or interviews. Direct evidence of learning outcomes generally is accorded more credibility than indirect evidence, and all board members should be aware that accreditation now requires at least one form of direct assessment to be used by all institutions for each claimed learning outcome.

Second, assessment can be undertaken using specially designed and deployed methods that are applied *outside* the normal teaching-learning context—special examinations, surveys, behavioral inventories, for example. Alternatively, such evidence can be developed by looking at *existing* student work—portfolios, work samples, observations of clinical practice, for example—from a more comprehensive or developmental perspective. Using naturally occurring examples of student work has the advantage of generating evidence without requiring either special instruments or special attention to ensuring student motivation to perform. But the abilities that naturally occurring evidence reveals may not completely correspond to the learning outcomes of interest. For example, observation of student performance in a clinical experience in a health-related field may indeed be authentic and unobtrusive. But the clinical encounter itself may not generate an opportunity for the student to reveal an important area of knowledge and skill—for example, how to respond to an emergency situation.

As they review assessment results, members of the academic affairs committee should know that there are substantial advantages to using naturally occurring assessment opportunities that are built directly into the curriculum. But they also should be aware that specially constructed examinations or demonstrations administered outside the curriculum and capable of being compared across institutions or

programs may be more comprehensive and useful under a different set
of circumstances.

The following are among the most common assessment methods
used by colleges and universities, together with their most important
advantages and challenges:

- *Examinations.* Examinations are the approach most commonly associated with the assessment of student-learning outcomes. Standardized
  multiple-choice tests are familiar to board members, and their results
  typically are used to compare institutions or programs. But faculty-con-
  structed examinations administered in class or as capstone demonstrations of mastery at the completion of a program can be equally valuable
  as evidence of attainment if they are deliberately constructed around
  a defined set of learning outcomes. Evidence based on examinations
  of either kind is direct and usually is reliably comparable across settings; it thus tends to be highly credible for external stakeholders. But
  examinations sometimes are limited in their ability to assess mastery
  or deeper forms of learning, especially if they are confined to "multiple
  choice" formats.

- *Tasks and demonstrations.* Tasks and demonstrations require
  students to directly deploy knowledge and skills in a particular setting
  to provide evidence of a desired level of performance. They may be
  deliberately constructed to generate such evidence (for example, a proof
  in mathematics or an engineering design), or they may occur naturally
  in the course of a learning experience when a particular situation arises
  (for example, an internship or clinical encounter). Evidence based
  on such situations is direct, but it also may be difficult to interpret
  consistently. As a result, effective use of these approaches as credible
  evidence of attainment requires developing and deploying carefully
  designed interpretive tools such as scoring guides or "rubrics" that
  describe each level of desired performance in some detail.

- *Student work.* This broad category of evidence potentially includes
  all of the "work products" generated naturally by students in a particular course of study, including written assignments, examinations, problems, laboratory reports, and field or clinical performances. Although
  such evidence has the advantage of having already been collected, a
  great deal of effort usually is involved in meaningfully assembling and
  interpreting it. As a result, most institutions using this approach sample
  such work products, then apply scoring guides or rubrics to draw conclusions about attainment.

  Probably the most common method for assembling student work is
  the *portfolio*, in which selected examples of a given student's work are
  chosen and examined together. Portfolios may be constructed analyti-
  cally—for example, choosing one or two pieces of work deliberately to

serve as illustrations of a given outcome. They also may be constructed to reflect development over time by including pieces of work that exemplify the same outcome at different stages of a student's academic career. Finally, scoring criteria can be built directly into the grading process and the results aggregated for later interpretation.

- *Behavioral outcomes.* Student behaviors before and after attendance can provide useful indirect-assessment information. For students in career-preparation programs, for example, placement and advancement in their field of study commonly is used as a measure of program success, as is participation in graduate study or continuing professional development. Other later behaviors frequently claimed as success measures for both institutions and programs include civic behaviors such as voting and volunteering, lifestyle behaviors such as health and consumption habits, or social and geographic mobility, all of which are related to intended outcomes. In most cases, such evidence is collected by surveys of graduates and former students.

- *Self-reporting.* A final method of obtaining indirect evidence about the attainment of student-learning outcomes is through the testimony of students themselves. Most commonly, students or graduates simply are asked to rate their own current levels of knowledge or skill across a set of areas that correspond to the learning outcomes in question. Most self-reports are collected by means of questionnaires, but alternative methods include telephone or individual interviews and focus groups. A debate continues about the validity and reliability of self-reports as proxy measures of actual student attainment, though considerable research has established consistent positive relationships between actual and claimed attainment. Self-reports generally are more credible for student behaviors, though these are only indirectly related to learning outcomes. Self-reports also are the only method available for obtaining evidence on such non-cognitive outcomes as attitudes, beliefs, or dispositions. Finally, evidence based on self-reports is commonly relied upon because of the ease and efficiency with which such information can be collected.

    Significantly, training in how to design any of these assessment approaches or to interpret the resulting data typically is not a part of the graduate preparation of most college faculty members. As a result, members of the academic affairs committee should ask explicitly about the institution's efforts to ensure that faculty members are being supported in their efforts to develop assessable learning-outcomes statements and to design effective methods to gather evidence of student achievement. Some of this support may be provided through a campus institute or a faculty development center. Assembling relevant publications on how to construct effective assessments and underwriting faculty attendance at assessment workshops also may be worthwhile.

The form of support is less important than the fact that attention is being paid to this nearly universal need for faculty development in assessment.

3. ***Are we benchmarking performance against external standards?*** Many institutional assessment programs now include at least a few sources of evidence that may be compared across institutions or against national norms. There are several reasons for this. First, comparative performance increasingly is being raised as a part of demands for increased accountability. States such as Tennessee and South Dakota require comparative performance on standardized tests for public colleges and universities, just as they do in elementary and secondary schools. Other states are likely to join them. Institutional accrediting organizations also are rapidly moving in the direction of asking institutions how their assessment results compare with some external standard.

At least as important from the board's perspective, external benchmarks of performance on learning outcomes can help the institution determine its areas of comparative advantage against peer institutions or against those with which it competes for students. And in some areas, institutions have used comparative assessment results of several kinds in their student recruitment campaigns.

Members of the academic affairs committee will want to be aware of the kinds of external benchmarks that are available. A first source is the array of nationally normed standardized achievement tests. Several testing companies have developed such examinations especially for program and institutional evaluation in higher education, and a number of institutions use them periodically to see how their students stack up against national performance levels and to calibrate their own, locally developed assessment approaches. Some of these examinations, such as ACT's Collegiate Assessment of Academic Proficiency (CAAP) or the Educational Testing Service's Measure of Academic Proficiency and Progress (MAPP), assess general skills such as writing, critical thinking, and problem solving. These established examinations recently have been joined by a non-multiple-choice general intellectual skills examination based on real-world tasks called the Collegiate Learning Assessment (CLA) marketed by the Council on Aid to Education.

Other national assessments assess performance in specific fields of study. For example, ETS offers Major Field Achievement Tests (MFAT) in 15 fields, based on their well-known Graduate Record Examinations (GREs). All of these examinations allow institutions to compare the performance of their students against national norms, and many allow comparisons against tailored comparison groups selected by institutions themselves.

Despite the ready use of examinations in benchmarking, committee members should know that there are many drawbacks to them. Because their content is determined externally, it may not match the content of the curriculum actually being taught at the institution. And because performance on these examinations does not usually count toward a grade, students may not be even inclined to take them or try their best if they do. What's more, faculty may be wary of such examinations because of suspicion that they do not test authentic mastery of student abilities in sufficient depth. Consequently, board members should refrain from advocating specific approaches, though they may be attracted to standardized testing in principle. In their regular reviews of assessment results, members of the academic affairs committee should ask whether any such benchmarking examinations have been considered. If such exams have been considered and rejected, committee members should probe and discuss specific reasons why this is the case.

Another source of external benchmarks is the aggregate set of results of the licensure and certification examinations typically taken by students in professional programs. These are especially common in the health professions but also show up in such fields as accounting, engineering, and teacher education. States frequently compile pass-rates on such examinations, and institutions may use these as institutional performance measures and as comparisons with national or state norms and with the results of other institutions. Members of the academic affairs committee should monitor which examinations are taken by the institution's graduates and how the graduates perform. But they should be aware that performance on such examinations—as on virtually all examinations—depends a lot on student background and academic aptitude. As a result, they should ask academic administrators how best to interpret and use the results.

Additionally, some institutions have formed data-sharing consortia of their own to obtain external benchmarks for their assessments. These are voluntary groups of reasonably similar institutions that arrange to share results on common assessments—generally on a confidential basis—to assist them in their own program improvement efforts. Most of these use the kinds of common examinations already described, but some have developed their own. Institutional consortia also can be helpful in aligning locally designed assessments by arranging for faculty at different institutions to review one another's assessment methods, scoring rubrics, and standards. Some institutions have even provided one another's programs with "external examiners" to look at student performance on a selected basis to see whether academic standards are comparable across institutions. Committee members should recognize that establishing such partnerships is a significant investment. But if no other appropriate ways are available to establish external points of comparison for the institution's assessment efforts, board members certainly may ask whether academic leaders and faculty have considered this route.

Finally, board and committee members should remember that not everything can or should be benchmarked to an external standard.

Establishing valid external points of comparison always is tricky, and the process should not be approached mechanically or universally. It is completely appropriate that most assessment methods be developed locally and not be tied to any such standard. If the primary goal of assessment is program improvement, it is far more important that the assessments being used fit the program's goals and context than whether they are externally benchmarked. But it certainly is important for the board periodically to ask the more general question of how the administration assures itself that the assessment results it obtains are adequate and appropriate.

4. *Who is responsible for assessment, and how is it accomplished?* Institutional assessment programs should also have a clear organizational structure on campus, with appropriate lines of responsibility and accountability. Because the board is responsible for ensuring that appropriate management structures are in place for assuring academic quality, it is part of the board's business to know what this structure looks like. Just as important, the fact that the institution has a visible structure for assessment—something that can actually be looked at during a campus visit—is becoming increasingly important in accreditation reviews. Once again, the academic affairs committee typically will be familiar with this organizational structure, and its members periodically should ask academic leaders whether it is appropriately resourced and functioning properly.

That said, there is no single approach to organizing assessment that fits the needs and contexts of all colleges and universities. Virtually all have an assessment committee charged with general oversight of the assessment function. Sometimes this committee is a formal part of the faculty governance structure—usually as a subcommittee of the academic planning or strategic planning committee—but sometimes it is part of the administrative committee structure that is advisory to the chief academic officer. Either choice is reasonable, depending upon the institution's circumstances. But because assessment is fundamentally a faculty responsibility, the membership and organization of the committee should clearly signal that faculty have the leading role in developing the assessment process and seeing that it is carried out properly. Board members should know the reasons why oversight of the assessment function is organized the way it is and should be assured that this governance structure has significant faculty voice and is not simply run by the administration.

Growing numbers of colleges and universities also are establishing assessment offices to assist the faculty in designing and administering assessments. Generally, these are staffed by one or more individuals with a background in testing and measurement, psychology, or the social sciences drawn from either outside the institution or from its own faculty. In some cases, this position is housed in and coordinated by a faculty development or teaching and learning center. In other cases, dedicated assessment staffing is added to the office of institutional research. Again, there is no right answer to the question of how best to create an organizational support structure for the necessarily decentralized process of assessment, which relies on the efforts of individual academic departments to do most of the work. But board members, and particularly members of the academic affairs committee, should know what resources are in place, who is responsible for them, and the reasons for these particular arrangements.

5. ***How do we use assessment results?*** Perhaps the biggest challenge facing campus assessment efforts is how to harness the resulting evidence to improve teaching and learning. This may come as a surprise to board members because continuous improvement is supposed to be a principal reason for doing assessment in the first place. But all too often, institutions first become engaged in assessment because of external requirements and, in the press of implementation, never systematically "close the loop" by carefully considering the implications of what they find and acting accordingly. Allowing this to happen is a mistake. Accreditors, for example, are not looking for a set of assessment procedures so much as they are seeking an institutional *culture* of evidence-based management that emphasizes action as well as data collection. And even if external accountability requirements were not present, running an expensive assessment process without using the results it generates is simply a waste of resources. Both scenarios merit watching by board members.

In asking academic administrators how and where they use assessment results, board members should recognize that there are a number of places where they might expect to see such applications. One is as part of the performance indicator system that many institutions have established to monitor their condition and effectiveness. Some colleges and universities include such measures as performance on externally benchmarked examinations, selected alumni survey results, or in-field job-placement rates on the "dashboards" they have created to track their performance. This is one of the most important connections for boards to ask about because such dashboards are intended to provide guidance about strategic direction and to track progress on established institutional priorities—priorities that the board at minimum has reviewed and approved or, preferably, helped establish in the first place.

Another potential area for application is in program or departmental review. Many institutions have established cyclical processes under which each academic program or department is examined every five to seven years—a process that usually involves a brief self-study and a systematic examination by an internal review panel (see Chapter 5). Increasingly, institutions are including an explicit assessment component in their program-review processes because the familiar framework of program review provides a ready-made opportunity to assemble and consider program-level assessment results.

Some institutions do not have an established program-review process around which to organize the assessment process. Most that do not have such a process use a specially devised program-level assessment reporting mechanism through which each department presents an annual or biennial description of how it gathers assessment evidence, what it has found in the latest cycle, and how the results have been used. Regardless, academic affairs committees provide a natural venue for examining program-level assessment results and discussing their implications with academic and faculty leaders. Members of the committee should ask specifically about the utilization component of these program-level reports, just as they should ask about how the results of surveys or of general education assessments have been used. Committee members should be especially interested in how this information can help inform strategic decisions. They might ask, for example, which of the programs provide good opportunities for expansion, or which programs that are especially important to the institution's mission are underperforming and therefore need attention and investment.

A third possible application of assessment results is in the budgeting process. Although most internal budgetary decisions are driven by established expenditure commitments, every institution engages in some form of "strategic budgeting" through which additional resources are allocated to support new strategic initiatives and needs. In their involvement with strategic planning, boards are involved in setting and approving the priorities used to guide such expenditures and rely on institutional leaders to provide the specific evidence of effectiveness to help identify these priorities. Academic affairs committees, in turn, may be more directly involved in setting strategic investment priorities for academic programs, for improving instruction, or for faculty development. Assessment evidence can prove especially important in these deliberations because it can clearly identify programmatic or instructional strengths on which to build or shortcomings in teaching and learning that need attention.

Finally, assessment results can be applied in student recruitment—an application that that has been prominently exploited as a marketing advantage by for-profit institutions in the realm of job placement and licensure passage. Board members should ask what assessment results can say about particular areas of success for graduates and how this information might help the institution's efforts to better position itself in an increasingly competitive market. These are all venues where boards might expect to see assessment results being used by institutional leaders, and board members should ask about such information if they do not see it. But most important, they should ensure that assessment results in all of these applications being used *strategically*—to help identify opportunities for investment that will further leverage institutional mission.

As a final point, boards should ask that the assessment process is itself periodically assessed to see whether it is organized appropriately, whether its methods of gathering evidence of student achievement are sound and appropriate, and whether its results are usable and being used. Although assessment programs are relatively new at most campuses, it is easy for those responsible for them to fall into a routine and become complacent. Every institution periodically should take a systematic look at its entire assessment operation—perhaps once every five years—to ensure that it is working as planned and to suggest enhancements or deletions. In this regard, academic affairs committees might make it a particular point to ask academic leaders each year about what is working well in assessment, what challenges have been encountered, and what could be improved.

# CHAPTER 3

# Retention, Graduation, and Student "Flow"

In an era of constrained financial resources, maintaining enrollment is of paramount importance to colleges and universities. Equally pressing are public concerns about the "educational pipeline" and the need to raise the success rates of students drawn from all backgrounds. In response, institutions are devoting greater attention to monitoring and shaping the characteristics of their undergraduate student bodies. Recruitment programs are being more carefully targeted to boost the probability that a given student will complete the program, and retention programs are being developed with much greater sensitivity to the need for different kinds of advising and intervention strategies for different kinds of students.

Nevertheless, an average of only 54.3 percent of entering four-year college freshmen complete their programs within six years and fewer than a third of entering two-year college students do so within three years, according to the National Center for Education Statistics. Board members need to understand, however, that such statistics do not tell the whole story about the complex phenomenon of student flow through the nation's higher education system.

First, these statistics are limited to students who enroll full-time and who are attending college for the first time. Given the high levels of part-time enrollments typical of many institutions and the equally high levels of new transfers in many others, these statistics may be only partially representative. For some community colleges, full-time, first-time students may comprise fewer than 10 percent of any entering group. These numbers also do not take into account the growing trend of students attending multiple institutions in pursuit of a degree. More than 60 percent of students who ultimately earn a bachelor's degree attended two or more institutions to do so (almost 20 percent attended three or more), according to a U.S. Department of Education study. On the one hand, this growing "enrollment swirl" tends to depress the graduation rates of individual institutions. But on the other hand, more frequent transfer tends to increase the overall rate of baccalaureate attainment. Some studies, for example, suggest that about 70 percent of those who enter college will have earned a bachelor's degree somewhere by the time they are 25.

These figures suggest just how complicated it is to determine patterns of student flow at the institutional level. Yet doing so is a crucial part of academic quality management. In addition to the financial implications of student dropouts, student success is an important indicator of the overall quality of an academic program. If students who are otherwise academically qualified are leaving in large numbers, there is surely a problem present that ought to be looked at even though the surviving graduates perform well.

Furthermore, graduation rates have become the single most common institutional performance measure now used in higher education—in many ways defining the reputations of all but the most selective institutions. Virtually all states require these rates to be reported for public institutions, and the federal Student Right to Know and Campus Security Act requires all institutions to disclose these rates to prospective students and their parents. Examining graduation rates and the reasons behind them also are becoming prominent topics in institutional accreditation reviews. For all these reasons, boards need to know how the institution is performing on such measures, and they must be assured that academic administrators have the information they need about student flow into and through the institution to enable them to intervene to increase student success rates.

# The Basics.

Retention and graduation statistics are calculated from information maintained in every institution's student registration system and typically are generated by the registrar or institutional research office. All colleges and universities are required by law to report to the federal government three-year or six-year graduation rates for full-time, first-time students, compiled according to a standard methodology and broken down by gender and by race/ethnicity. All such statistics are calculated on a so-called "cohort" basis. This means that a group of entering students are selected at a particular point in time (in the case of federal reporting, students who entered the institution for the first time in the fall term) and are tracked to a point in time six years later (or three, in the case of community colleges) to determine whether they have earned a degree. The basic graduation rate is then calculated by dividing those members of the original group who have completed a degree within this designated period by the total number who originally started. Retention-rate calculations are similar and generally are calculated for first-year students returning for a second year.

When interpreting the retention and graduation statistics provided by institutional leaders, board members should know what generally influences the numbers. The most important drivers of overall retention and graduation are institutional selectivity and student academic ability. All other things equal, highly selective institutions will significantly outperform institutions that have open admissions, and within a given institution, students with higher SAT or ACT scores are more likely to be retained than their counterparts with lower scores. Private institutions also generally have higher retention rates than public institutions (63 percent versus 52 percent). Other factors that tend to be positively related to higher retention and graduation rates are full-time continuous attendance, direct entry out of high school, and sufficient financial-aid support. Factors that tend to be negatively related to higher rates are nontraditional student characteristics (older, part-time), minority status (especially black and Hispanic), lower income, and first-generation college attendance.

It is important to emphasize that demographics is not destiny in these matters. Many institutions of modest selectivity retain students at higher rates than their peers, while others fail to retain their brightest students. Institutional commitments and actions matter a lot in the area of student success; *all* institutions can improve their performance. Board attention to this issue can help ensure that institutional leaders are paying attention to this.

This point is especially important because recent research on understanding student retention and success emphasizes the preeminent roles of presidential leadership and institutional culture in promoting higher graduation rates.[1] Exemplary institutions not only have the proper programs and resources in place, they are also characterized by presidents who visibly call attention to the institution's commitment to help students succeed. Partly as a result of vigorous and visible presidential leadership, these campuses display a proactive readiness to help students who are having difficulty succeeding; it is part of the way faculty and staff do their everyday work. Boards should raise these matters explicitly when graduation and retention statistics are reported to them because trustees are uniquely positioned to ensure presidential attention. Finally, the institutions that are most effective in retaining students take evidence seriously and have developed sophisticated ways of analyzing available data about student flow to understand how particular kinds of students are experiencing the institution, what can be done to improve these experiences, and how to monitor the progress and effectiveness of efforts to improve student success. As in all other areas of academic quality assurance, boards should make sure these data resources are in place and are being used.

# Questions for Boards to Consider.

Because understanding the nuances of statistics about student success is a challenge, board members should be careful not to over-interpret such measures. Understanding what goes into them and what they really mean is important, however. Similarly, managing student flow to create the right kinds of efficiencies and to intervene effectively to maximize student success is a job faculty and staff need to be doing every day—and presidents

---

1   See Kuh, George D.; Kinzie, Jillian; Schuh, John H.; Whitt, Elizabeth J.; and Associates (2005). *Student Success in College*. San Francisco: Jossey-Bass. See also AASCU (2005). *The Graduation Rate Outcomes Project*. Washington, D.C.: American Association of State Colleges and Universities.

need to motivate them to continue. Once boards are assured that the right things are being done, they need to ask for periodic reports on effectiveness and stay out of the way. But there definitely are some "big picture" questions in this arena that board members ought to ask.

1. ***What are our basic indicators of student progression and success?*** Boards need to ensure that the institution's leaders are monitoring retention and graduation rates. All institutions must provide the federal government with such statistics make them available to prospective students and their parents through Web sites, catalogues, or recruiting publications. But this does not mean that leaders are really looking at these numbers, determining what they mean, and tailoring active and continuous steps to improve performance. At many institutions, such reporting is simply a routine operational task but goes no farther. Boards can prevent complacency by asking that results of the federal Graduation Rate Survey (GRS) be reported to them each year along with more conventional statistics such as admissions and enrollment numbers. They also should know how and where the required statistics are being disclosed to stakeholders. More important, they should ask administrators to discuss with them the institution's results and the implications.

In asking such questions, boards are signaling the importance they attach to the institution's efforts to improve student success. But they probably will discover that there are more effective ways to measure the institution's success in this arena than the federally mandated statistics. As noted earlier, these measures may leave out substantial proportions of the institution's entering students, including those who do not enroll full-time and those who have transferred in. For community colleges, moreover, many students are successful because they transfer to a four-year institution before they earn a degree. As a result, boards should ask administrators what indicators *they* use in monitoring overall student success and in managing their efforts to improve it. If these measures are different from those that are publicly reported, boards need to know the reasons why and what additional insights these measures provide.

Many of these discussions may take place in the academic affairs committee. This is the natural venue when measures of student flow bear on the curriculum and patterns of student course-taking or academic behavior. But because retention also is an aspect of enrollment management, these topics may be the purview of board committees that deal with competitiveness, marketing, or student affairs. Just as it is difficult to assign issues concerning student progress to any one administrative office, it also is tough to limit these discussions to any given board committee. As a result, the board as a whole should ensure that presidents and senior administrators are paying attention.

Finally, on whatever basis the administration determines how well the institution is performing with respect to retention and program completion, boards ought to ask for an estimate of the *cost* of attrition.

All enrolled students reflect the institutional costs associated with recruiting them and ensuring that they will matriculate. If a given student leaves, another will need to be recruited to take his or her place. Every student who leaves represents lost tuition revenue (and for some institutions, state subsidies as well). Although it is conventional wisdom that it is easier to retain a current student than to recruit a new one, this may not be true at all institutions; in many cases, these costs cannot be calculated precisely. Presidents ought to be able to discuss with the board the broad financial consequences for the institution associated with students failing to complete their programs.

2. *How does our performance measure up?* Boards need to know something about the institution's comparative performance on retention and graduation measures. This means using publicly reported statistics obtained from the GRS or, for public institutions, comparative institutional statistics reported by the system office or state higher education coordinating board. As noted earlier, comparing institutional outcomes on these measures is tricky because performance will vary naturally based on institutional characteristics such as selectivity and program offerings as well as on student characteristics. Comparisons with national averages are not very helpful for this reason, making it far better to compare the institution's outcomes with those of institutions with similar characteristics.

One useful vehicle for making such comparisons is an online tool available from the Washington-based Education Trust. This Web site (*www.collegeresults.org*) automatically selects a set of peer institutions based on such characteristics as size, admissions test scores, minority and part-time enrollment, financial-aid need, and academic program offerings. It then generates displays that show how a selected institution stacks up against these peers with respect to graduation. The site also may be used to construct a set of peers on a more subjective, judgmental basis looking at specific institutional characteristics or combinations of characteristics. Board committees concerned with marketing or admissions may find this comparative information especially useful in discussions with institutional leaders—especially when discussing an institution's relative performance against its competitors. Consulting this site even once can be useful for board members, if only to make them aware of the considerable variation in retention and graduation rates across different kinds of colleges and universities.

Other sources of similar information include the AGB Benchmarking Service (*www.agb.org*) and the reports posted annually by state system or coordinating boards. Boards should ensure that administrators are aware of these sources of comparative information and should ask how they explain any differences in performance between the institution and its peers as well as any implications these differences might have for action.

### 3. *What does success look like for different kinds of students?*

Overall retention and graduation rates tell only a limited story about student success at any institution. Regardless of its general enrollment profile, every institution has not a single student body, but many—comprising different subgroups of students defined by different combinations of characteristics. While each institution is different in this respect, subpopulations that immediately come to mind are student athletes, adult or part-time students, students living in residence halls or off campus, commuter students, minority students, and students with known academic challenges. The board may be especially interested in students to whom the institution is providing institutional aid because it will want to be certain the institution is investing its own money as fully as possible in those most likely to succeed.

Each subpopulation may experience a different pattern of success as it moves through the institution. An overall graduation rate is simply the combination of these diverse subpopulation rates, which may differ from one another. In fact, institutions are frequently fooled into believing they have improved retention rates through improved programming when all they have really done is changed the enrollment proportions among various subpopulations that have different retention rates.

Consequently, board members need to ask how different kinds of students are faring in terms of retention and graduation. Federal reporting already requires institutions to break down retention and graduation rates by gender and race/ethnicity, so these rates should be readily available. But in addition to these, which types of students are experiencing the highest success rates and which the lowest? How much of a difference exists between these groups, and is it significant or substantive enough to worry about? What have been the trends over time with respect to these subgroup performances?

In asking these questions, it is important to explore the administration's own views of which subgroups are most important and how their experiences are likely to differ. Board members should be aware of the fact that successful intervention strategies usually differ for different kinds of students. "Best practice" institutions do not embark on "generic" retention efforts that treat everybody the same; instead, they recognize that student success requires careful coordination of a range of strategies targeted at different student populations, each of which has a particular set of retention challenges. The concept here is similar to the notion of "market segmentation," with which some board members already may be familiar through discussions about student recruitment. The board needs to determine that academic and student affairs leaders are thinking this way and are examining approaches that take subpopulation differences into account.

That said, there are a number of important distinctions to keep in mind when disaggregating these kinds of statistics. First, it is useful to know whether students who left the institution did so for academic or nonacademic reasons. A usual breakdown is whether a given student was in good academic standing during his or her last term of enrollment. Overall grade-point averages also are frequently used to make this distinction. While it is understandable that some students having academic difficulty may drop out, every student who leaves for nonacademic reasons represents a case that may have been preventable and raises questions about what might be done in the future to prevent such losses.

Second, it is useful to know not only which kinds of students dropped out but also when they did so. National statistics, as well as substantial research at the campus level, suggest that most students are at risk in their first year—frequently making the provisional decision to leave early in their first term, though they may not act on it right away. Their reasons include early bad experiences with services provided, perceived lack of fit with the institution and its culture, an inability to connect socially with anyone at the institution, and so forth. Reasons for later withdrawal in good academic standing—in the second or third year, for example—are much more likely to be programmatic. This might include an inability to find the right major (and its availability elsewhere) or a decision to switch programs or potential careers. Boards should ensure that administrators have made these basic distinctions in the way they are looking at retention data and are following up on the implied programmatic remedies.

4. *Who is accountable for student success, and what are we doing to improve our performance?* Student success is everybody's job, but it often is nobody's explicit responsibility. Student affairs staff are on the front lines of the effort, providing counseling, programming, financial aid, and a range of other services. But these services all too frequently are provided independently and with little guidance regarding an overarching goal.

Faculty are critical to the effort to foster student success as well, because students' academic advisement and classroom experiences crucially shape their impressions and attitudes during their first year of attendance. Isolated in individual classrooms, however, some faculty members deal only with "pieces" of students unless they also act as advisers. More important, some faculty members do not see student retention as part of their jobs because they are focused strictly on teaching and research in their discipline.

Athletics directors also are deeply concerned about retention and success for student athletes. The National Collegiate Athletic Association directly monitors graduation rates for student athletes, and institutions can lose eligibility if performance is too low. Some collegiate athletics departments have developed their own exemplary academic and counseling support programs that other parties on campus may learn from.

Finally, every other employee at the institution may have a role to play—groundskeepers, maintenance workers, food service employees, bursar's clerks, or campus security—because any of them may touch, or fail to touch, students in a meaningful way. Any of these individuals may affect a particular student's success, but they have to know how to behave appropriately in their roles, and somebody must be responsible for seeing that they do.

Presidents are crucial in building a campus oriented toward student success. Boards therefore need to ensure that active efforts to retain and graduate students are near the top of the president's agenda. But they also need to know the president's thinking about how the institution is *organized* to carry out this vital task. At some institutions, organizational responsibility for student success is explicitly located in a particular office or individual. At others, it is assumed to be part of the mission of every academic department and support unit, with contributions to retention and student success programming made a visible part of the accountability review for chairs and directors, and actively overseen by the appropriate vice presidents. There is no "right" recipe for how to do this, and much depends on history, campus culture, and presidential leadership style. But board members need to know how it is done on their campus, the reasons for doing it this way, and whether or not it is working.

At the same time, boards should be broadly familiar with the kinds of student success programs that have proved effective across multiple settings. Among the most prominent are the following:

- First-year experience programs that begin with new-student orientation and continue throughout a student's first term or year, involving special programming to help students acclimate to college, learn to use academic resources such as the library, develop good study and work habits, and foster engagement through strong peer relationships;

- Early assessment of student's basic skills, followed by effective placement and remediation if deficiencies are detected;

- Academic "early warning" systems that provide faculty with a channel to quickly telegraph student difficulties to advisement or student affairs staff who can promptly intervene to provide the necessary help;

- Proactive student advisement arrangements that help students internalize what is expected of them and that provide them with clear "pathways" through the curriculum that are effective for learning and that students understand;

- Flexible and understandable procedures for providing necessary services such as financial aid and registration;

- Integrated student-service centers that provide "one-stop shopping" for such services as advising, counseling, financial aid, registration, tutoring, academic support, and health care; and

- Specific curricular features such as "learning communities" that involve groups of students taking common content-linked coursework their first year, internships and other service-learning opportunities, and student research programs that promote frequent and meaningful contact between faculty and students.

Numerous reviews have cited such practices as being effective in increasing student success, and boards should be in a position to recognize them as such. But it is important to stress that these sources also emphasize that "sound programming" alone is not sufficient to guarantee success. They must instead be developed and delivered in the nexus of a campus culture that emphasizes high expectations for students, a belief that any student admitted can succeed in meeting these expectations, and a prevailing attitude among faculty and staff that helping all students to achieve their potential is an integral part of their everyday work.

Building a culture of student success is of strategic importance both because of the negative fiscal impact of low graduation rates and because poor performance shapes public and marketplace perceptions of the institution's quality. Active presidential commitment and leadership are crucial for fostering such a culture. Active board interest in the reality behind graduation and retention statistics may help busy presidents keep student success near the top of their agendas.

# CHAPTER 4

# Listening to Stakeholders and "Customers"

It should seem natural to most board members that colleges and universities periodically survey their students and alumni. Seeking customer feedback, of course, is a practice of every sound business. But the results of such evidence gathering, done right, also can provide an important new source of information for academic quality assurance and improvement. To be sure, using the term "customer" in connection with students will not always be welcome among academics. Yet in some important ways, this is exactly what students are, so it is appropriate to look at them in this way. Most students choose which college to attend, and their satisfaction as expressed to family and friends may be decisive in influencing their peers to make the same choice. Students are direct "consumers" of the many services provided by colleges and universities—bookstores, food services, and parking—and they are the best experts on their satisfaction with these services. They also participate in a range of processes run by the institution such as registration and financial aid where feedback may be important.

Academics have a point when they argue that viewing students only as customers may be a wrong-headed way to look at the teaching and learning process. Here, to stretch the "production process" analogy a bit, students may be more like the "raw materials" that are transformed by what the institution does to yield a "value added" product (a product, as a business executive once pointed out, that can talk about the process). Further stretching the analogy in a way more amenable to the views of educators, students also are "co-producers" and "managers" of their own learning. *They* are the ones that make important decisions about how much time to spend on various kinds of learning activities and how they actually will use the learning resources the institution puts at their disposal.

Knowing how students do this—the kinds of experiences they seek and the decisions they make—often is critical to understanding what is really happening in the teaching and learning process. This may be an especially salient topic for the board's academic affairs committee because its members will want to hear the student perspective as well as that of the faculty. Evidence drawn from student surveys is important in determining "hidden" student motivations and experiences, so committee members should know how to look at such evidence appropriately.

# The Basics.

Although many surveys typically are administered to students by certain campus offices and services, most institutions mount a few central survey efforts aimed at current students or alumni on a regular basis. These generally are run by the student affairs office or, if the institution has one, the office of institutional research. Most institutions develop their own surveys, but more and more also are participating in one or more national surveys to enable comparative benchmarking. Among the most prominent are the following:

- *The Freshman Survey offered by the Cooperative Institutional Research Program (CIRP).* Based at UCLA, the longest running student-survey effort in higher education generally makes national news about the attitudes and characteristics of the nation's entering freshman class. Items on this survey are comprehensive and range from family background to values and political views to academic experiences in high school to perceived preparation levels. CIRP also conducts a follow-up survey containing parallel items for graduates a decade after their freshman year.

- *The National Survey of Student Engagement (NSSE).* Based at Indiana University, NSSE ("Nessie") explicitly examines experiences and curricular features that prior research has demonstrated to be associated with substantive gains in learning—factors such as frequent and meaningful student-faculty contact, time spent studying and in other academic pursuits, active and experience-based learning opportunities, and a supportive campus environment. The survey is administered simultaneously to samples of end-of-year freshmen and about-to-graduate seniors. A parallel survey effort for two-year colleges is the Community College Survey of Student Engagement (CCSSE), based at the University of Texas, Austin.

- *The College Student Experience Questionnaire (CSEQ).* Also based at Indiana University, this survey provides a more in-depth look at student academic experiences by looking explicitly at the use of various academic resources provided by the institution. This includes student use of the library, participation in different kinds of courses or out-of-class learning experiences, and academic interaction with the faculty and their peers. The survey is founded on the notion of "quality of effort"—the level and type of investment that students exhibit in their academic work.

- *The Noel-Levitz Student Satisfaction Inventory.* Noel-Levitz is an independent consulting firm specializing in retention work. It offers a series of surveys that ask students to evaluate the services they receive in terms of their importance to them and how well they believe they are being served. The resulting "performance gap" between importance and satisfaction ratings is the primary analytical tool used in interpreting results.

- **The Evaluation Survey Service (ESS) offered by ACT.** This long-standing family of surveys addresses general college experiences, satisfaction with services and academic offerings, and self-assessments on a range of student outcomes. Different editions of the survey are tailored for administration to new students, continuing students, about-to-graduate students, and recent alumni.

- **Your First College Year.** This end-of-freshman year survey offered through UCLA examines first-year college experiences that research has demonstrated to be associated with retention of first-year students. It was designed in conjunction with the nationally recognized Center on the First College Year based at Brevard College in North Carolina and was developed in partnership with the long-standing program of research on the freshman year experience at the University of South Carolina.

All of these national surveys can be administered on a consortium basis with other institutions, and all provide flexible reports involving peer comparisons. All of them also allow institutions to add questions of their own design, which are scored along with the regular items and fed back to the institution. These advantages are substantial, and if the institution has never used one of them for benchmarking, board members should ask why. There are many legitimate reasons for not doing so, ranging from cost to inappropriate survey content in the context of the institution's mission. But raising this question makes this important choice explicit.

Board and committee members also should be generally aware of the ways in which such surveys typically are administered. While the traditional means is through the mail, the Web is increasingly being used as a survey medium because it is inexpensive and because responses arrive in electronic form. Also, to cut costs, many survey managers administer surveys to just a sample of the target student population instead of sending them to all students. Like public-opinion polling, sampling can yield an accurate pattern of overall response at a fairly low cost, but the results are accurate only within a specified margin of error (usually about 3 percent to 5 percent). The smaller the sample, the more difficult it becomes to break down accurately the responses of increasingly smaller subgroups.

Interpreting survey results is mostly about internal comparisons, trends in results over time, and benchmarked comparisons with other institutions. This is because the overall response to a particular survey item may have as much to do with how the question is worded than any underlying condition. Interpreting survey results, then, is generally about looking for patterns of high and low scores across different survey questions or across different surveyed populations. Finally, much less frequently, surveys are supplemented by qualitative study methods such as focus groups and interviews. These usually are accomplished in conjunction with surveys to probe student opinion more deeply.

# Questions for Boards to Consider.

As with other areas, the board's first concern in the realm of "customer feedback" is to ensure that the institution has such mechanisms in place. A second obvious "bottom line" is to determine whether the basic pattern of response indicates overall satisfaction among students and stakeholders and, if problems are apparent, that the administration has a reasonable plan to address them. Beyond these basic fiduciary concerns, questions that board members might appropriately ask in this realm—especially in the academic affairs committee—include the following:

1.  ***What do student responses tell us about the quality of their academic experiences?*** As "customers," students naturally will have a lot to report about their satisfaction with direct services, and board members should be sure that the administration is listening. But at a deeper level, boards should inquire about the extent to which student surveys are directed at the essential question of academic quality. This may be a particularly appropriate topic for the academic affairs committee to take up, discuss with academic leaders, and report on to the full board.

    A first point here is the nature of the questions students are asked. Surveys such as NSSE, CCSSE, and CSEQ are explicitly designed to solicit students' testimony about the quality of their academic experiences. If institutions use their own surveys, it is appropriate to ask academic administrations about the extent to which they look at such matters as experiences with faculty, student engagement with academic work, and the extent to which they encounter "good practices" in teaching and learning (these practices include collaborative work, active and "hands-on" learning experiences, and service or community-based learning).

    Moreover, as with the results of learning assessments and graduation rates, student testimony about academic quality will differ from one student population to another. It is therefore useful for committee members to know not only about the overall pattern of response but also about any major differences in perceptions or experience that may be evident among different kinds of students. Overall averages can be deceptive here. For example, survey results may tell us that the average student spends 12.5 hours per week in out-of-class academic activities such as doing assigned reading, writing papers, completing problem sets, or using the library. But within this average, there may be a considerable range of behavior. How many students are spending only an hour or two on these activities, or no time at all? And if substantial numbers of under-engaged students are out there, what are their characteristics?

While the academic affairs committee may look at such results and engage academic leaders in active dialogue about what they should do when survey results suggest lack of engagement, the full board needs to be assured that administrators are probing below the surface to determine whether different patterns of student experience are present.

Student survey results are also much more powerful when they can be linked to other kinds of information about student learning experiences. For example, most student surveys allow institutions the option of including a student identification number or similar unique identifier that can provide a link to other sources of information. Linked to the student's transcript, for example, this allows student testimony about the quality of their experiences to be considered together with what classes they took, in what order they took them, when they declared a major, and similar behavioral information. Links to responses to past or future surveys, in turn, allows a look at how a given student's experience has changed over time. Using all three data points can generate powerful analyses of how students are moving through the institution's curriculum and what is happening to them at each stage. Again, this is a good topic to be raised and discussed periodically by the academic affairs committee.

Similarly, student testimony can be considered together with parallel information drawn from faculty or student affairs staff. The NSSE program, for instance, sponsors an additional survey, the Faculty Survey of Student Engagement (FSSE), which typically is completed by faculty at the same time students complete NSSE. This process allows exploration of the contrasts and areas of agreement between student and faculty perceptions of the learning experience. Many institutions using this approach have found faculty expectations of student time on task or levels of class preparation to be far in excess of what students actually say they are doing—a contrast that has provoked a good deal of discussion and reaction. A similar approach could be used with any of the student surveys an institution may be using.

As this last example makes clear, board members should recognize that one of the best uses of survey results is as a means of starting discussions among academic leaders and faculty about how learning is occurring and what may be hindering it. They also should be as concerned with the ways the administration is making use of these opportunities to stimulate reflective conversations about teaching and learning as they are about the results themselves.

2. ***How confident can we be about what we've found?*** On the face of it, students' testimony about their experiences seems compelling. After all, it is *their* experiences, and their reports should be credible. But if the academic affairs committee begins to delve deeply into student survey results in dialogue with academic and student affairs leaders, its members also should be wary of jumping to conclusions about what student responses to survey questions really mean. More specifically, they should know the many ways in which the information that can be drawn from surveys is limited.

First, as noted earlier, most surveys are based on samples of students or alumni rather than the entire population. This means that they have a given margin of error at a given level of confidence, both of which depend upon the size of the sample. So a particular survey result—say 62 percent responding that they are "satisfied" or "very satisfied" with the advising they have received—will *really* mean something like: "We can be certain that 95 percent of the time between 57 percent and 67 percent of students feel this way."

Second, it is fairly certain that not all students who are asked to respond to a given survey actually do so—and the smaller the number of respondents, the greater the need for caution in evaluating the responses. Although some institutions are able to obtain response rates of 75 percent or more to student or alumni surveys, the vast majority of institutions do nowhere near so well. The national response rate for the NSSE survey, which is administered using some of the most sophisticated current survey techniques, is 42 percent, and overall student survey response rates have been declining over the past decade. Receiving a low response rate does not necessarily compromise results, but it does introduce additional uncertainty about how to interpret them. If more women responded than men (which typically is the case), the result may not change if men and women feel the same way about the question being asked. But if they don't, the overall result may be skewed toward the female point of view.

Taken together, these two conditions inherent to all surveys suggest caution in interpreting results. When examining evidence based on surveys, board and committee members always should be provided with the margin of error and level of confidence associated with the results. They also should be aware of the response rate to the survey and what the analysts presenting it can tell them about how any differences in response rates among different kinds of students might affect interpretation. Finally, committee members should look for noticeable differences in responses across different kinds of questions or different kinds of respondents.

A deeper issue of interpretation is the extent to which student testimony is trustworthy, especially when students are telling us about how much they have learned. Numerous studies indicate that student self-reports about learning are in fact correlated with direct measures of their learning, but these correlations are far from perfect. This is why accrediting agencies these days insist on *direct* evidence about the attainment of learning outcomes of the kinds discussed in Chapter 2. But self-reports about learning gathered through student surveys can still be valuable to an institution as a cross-check on what direct assessment approaches are telling us.

Furthermore, if students report that they are *not* learning in a particular area, this may be important in its own right. Such a response may signal a problem in learning itself, indicate that the ability in question is not being addressed in the curriculum, or that the students don't understand what is meant. Research on this matter shows that students are far more credible witnesses of their *behaviors* associated with learning. They can usually tell us with fair accuracy how much they study, how much contact they have with faculty, and what their learning experiences are like. This makes it all the more important for the institution's analysts to ask about such matters beyond straightforward satisfaction when they seek student opinions. When surveying alumni, moreover, the amount of time between when they graduated and when their views are sought also can be important, especially if the institution has changed in some important ways in the interim; those who respond may be reporting on an institution that in some sense no longer exists.

For all these reasons, despite its efficiency and considerable utility, information drawn from surveys always must be treated with caution. Board and committee members should be aware of these caveats when considering survey results and should ask administrators and those presenting that data about their views regarding the limitations of the results and whether there is corroborating evidence from a different source.

3. ***How are we considering other stakeholder views?*** While students are the most obvious "stakeholders" for the institution, a range of additional individuals and entities consider the quality of academic offerings important. These may include employers, professional associations, community opinion leaders, other institutions that provide transfer or graduate-education destinations, and citizens of the region. It is important for boards and administrators to understand who these stakeholders are and how their perceptions potentially affect the institution. Consideration of their perceptions in particular may help determine priorities for determining what stakeholders think.

Gathering information from external constituencies can be difficult and expensive, so it is not something to do frequently if the constituency in question is marginal. Experience suggests that mailed surveys are not the best way to obtain feedback from external constituents because they tend to be busy people, and it is sometimes difficult for them to see the connection between the institution and what they do. As a result, a lot of initial contact and preparation is generally needed for such efforts to be successful. Area employers, for instance, may care a good deal about both the technical skills of graduates and more generic "employability" skills such as motivation, personal responsibility, and teamwork. But they are generally more comfortable talking about these matters directly with institutional representatives than filling out a survey. Successful institutions contact employers well in advance through letters or phone calls that explain why the institution wants their views and what will be done with the information. Other approaches include working through established channels such as chambers of commerce or local trade associations. Focus groups and direct face-to-face interviews in the interviewee's own place of business usually are the most effective methods for gathering the needed information.

Individual academic programs or departments may have established relationships with external stakeholders through program advisory committees. These generally are formed to advise on curriculum content, but their members increasingly are being recruited as "external assessors" to help program faculty determine the adequacy of student work. At the very least, these representatives should be asked directly about the kinds of knowledge and skills they are seeking in newly trained employees. And the basic concept of using such outside experts can be extended to non-vocational and professional disciplines, such as those in the arts and sciences, by recruiting external advisory groups composed of disciplinary faculty drawn from other institutions.

In sum, all board members should be broadly aware of the many ways in which the institution may be seeking student and stakeholder perceptions of academic need and effectiveness. Given the rising public profile of higher education, student and stakeholder input is an integral part of academic quality assurance, and boards should expect their institutions to be fully and appropriately engaged.

Members of the academic affairs committee should be more deeply engaged in reviewing the evidence generated about student and stakeholder perceptions, and they should work with academic and student affairs leaders to draw out and address any issues that may emerge. Are there patterns of dissatisfaction or systematic discontinuities in student-learning experiences that are significant enough to constitute a threat to the institution's long-term reputation or ability to attract the kinds of students it wants? Are there patterns of student experience that are especially positive and noteworthy that the institution might exploit more systematically in recruitment and marketing?

The broader perspective that board members bring to such discussions frequently is more effective in raising issues about what is happening to students and what is important to stakeholders than the narrower and self-interested perspective of academic leaders. As always, this does not mean that board members should forget the distinction between raising and pursuing strategic issues and micro-managing decisions about academic content or the details of student-affairs programming. But it does imply that trustees should judiciously examine presented evidence and raise the right questions to ensure that the institution's leadership is paying attention.

# CHAPTER 5

# Taking Stock of Program Assets

Every retail business needs to think about its product line. Some establishments are "convenience stores," serving a broad local market with a wide but shallow array of everyday wares. Others are "department stores," whose customers expect higher quality, greater selection, and an even broader range of available goods. Still others are "specialty outlets" that depend upon providing only a few kinds of products to a sufficient mass of customers to keep them in business.

Colleges and universities are a mix of these types with respect to their principal product—academic programs—and all three retail analogies are useful to stimulate thinking strategically about academic programs. In the turbulent world of market competition, moreover, corporations have learned that it is wise not to try to be top-notch in everything but to develop a set of well-researched strategic priorities that dictate the few areas where true quality lies, and where they should invest the most resources. This does not mean they divest themselves of all other businesses. These may be necessary to maintain for a variety of reasons ranging from strong local markets to the need to protect a brand or reputation. But it does imply careful planning to identify product strengths, weaknesses, and customer demands as well as differential investment in a few high-quality lines.

Although higher education institutions clearly differ from corporations or retail outlets, they need to engage in a similar kind of strategic thinking. And this is especially true when it comes to a college or university's "stock" of academic programs. Like department stores, most institutions are expected to maintain a given array of academic programs even though some of them are run at a loss. Everyone expects a college or university to have a physics department just as everyone entering a department store expects it to sell major appliances. In addition, colleges and universities create internal markets for teaching in a range of fields because of their general education requirements. There may be relatively few students majoring in English, for example, but every student who hopes to graduate has to take some English classes. Both these pressures keep most institutions from specializing in their best-reputed academic programs to the extent many retail businesses end up doing. But most colleges and universities also have some programs that are better than others and that they would be wise to further market and invest in to reinforce perceptions of quality. And most also have

41

*Making The Grade*

programs that they should consider phasing down or eliminating entirely.

These are all matters that academic administrators need to think about when reviewing their array of undergraduate programs. Addressing questions about the optimal size, configuration, and performance of these offerings is an important part of academic quality management and quality assurance. Boards need to assure themselves that the chief academic officer and senior academic staff are paying attention to these matters. And board members should be aware of some of the principles, tools, and evidence available for use in discharging these tasks.

## The Basics.

Every institution keeps (or should keep) an array of statistics that monitors the overall condition of its academic programs. Most of these are pretty straightforward—enrolled students by major, numbers of full-time and part-time faculty by rank or category, and classes taught or credits generated—and most boards are likely to receive these sorts of statistics from the institution's chief academic officer.

Examined over time, such statistics can paint a picture of the changing demands for instruction in relation to parallel changes in teaching assets. But actively managing academic programs demands a different way of looking at various statistics. As a result, many institutions construct regular performance ratios to analyze how particular programs are operating. When appropriate opportunities arise, members of the academic affairs committee should ask chief academic officers what kinds of measures they use to monitor program condition and performance on an ongoing basis, and what related issues may be arising.

Many colleges and universities also have established a system of academic program review. Most of these operate on a regular cycle, with each program examined every five to seven years. For public institutions, this sometimes occurs in common across all units in a system or state. While the pattern varies across institutions, most program reviews involve the compilation of a detailed statistical summary using various indicators, a written self-study prepared according to a standard protocol by the program's faculty, and an examination of both of these bodies of evidence by an internal peer-review team composed of academic staff and faculty from other disciplines. In some cases, external reviewers from the same field or discipline are included, and their independent reports are made part of the record.

These reviews are intended to be comprehensive and to suggest ways in which the program might be improved. Areas addressed by most review protocols, for instance, include an analysis of student demand and future need, enrollment trends, faculty background and preparation, other important resources such as equipment and space, curriculum coverage and structure, and teaching and research activities. Given the increasing attention paid to outcomes by accrediting organizations, such reviews now usually also devote a good deal of attention to results of assessments of student learning. And if the institution has programs that are independently accredited by programmatic accrediting organizations, their external review usually is built into the internal program review schedule to avoid duplication of effort.

Because the primary intent of program review is supposed to be academic improvement, a prominent part of the process is the recommendations for change that it generates. The majority of these originate with the faculty's self-study, indicating changes that faculty members themselves would like to make and that probably require new resources. This has earned the process some criticism because traditional academic program reviews almost never identify actions that might *save* resources, or programs that might be eliminated. Nevertheless, the process provides a welcome opportunity to check up on the institution's program array on a regular basis, and it can be especially helpful in quality assurance if external reviewers are included in the process.

Occasionally, colleges and universities will examine their entire array of academic offerings in depth simultaneously as part of a strategic planning or budgetary exercise. In contrast to the more common rolling cycle of program review in which information about at least some programs is several years out of date, this has the virtue of considering common current data and assessing the place and need of each academic program within the curriculum as a whole. Most institutions undertake such exercises only when under significant budgetary pressure, when the primary motive is to find something to cut in order to preserve (or even enhance) programs they consider high quality or mission-central. This is unfortunate because this kind of strategic look at the total configuration of academic programs may be useful regardless of the condition of the budget.

# Questions for Boards to Consider.

Examining how and how well academic programs are working is central to the task of academic management. As with any management task, boards should assure themselves that those responsible are taking it on and using the right tools. The most important questions board members should ask, therefore, are how the institution's academic leadership determines whether the right array of academic programs is in place and whether new programs should be added or existing programs discontinued. Academic affairs committees, in turn, may delve more deeply by asking whether the academic programs are operating efficiently and achieving intended objectives. In addition, when topics related to academic program effectiveness arise in the course of regular board discussion, board and committee members may wish to raise questions such as the following:

1. ***Do we have the right mix of programs?*** It is important for all
board members to understand that the natural rhythm of program
development at most colleges and universities is not entirely rational.
Unlike commercial enterprises, which generally prepare for the launch
of a new product with a good deal of research on customer demand, cost
of production, and marketability, most academic programs are developed because the faculty want to teach them and doing so will enhance
their reputation and that of the institution. If a new cadre of faculty is
hired with a specialization in a particular branch of cell biology, for
example, there likely will be new classes offered in this field, and the
program eventually may mushroom into a major. (This occurs most
often at the graduate level.) This process has been much parodied, but
it is not at all atypical.

And it is also not all bad. Academic entrepreneurship is what keeps
colleges and universities vital, and branching out into new fields of
instruction may well lead the institution in promising new scholarly directions. It may be equally useful, however, for board members—and particularly members of the academic affairs committee—to ask academic
leaders periodically how program inventories are monitored and managed.
There are several points to listen for when raising such questions.

The first and most important "program mix" question for boards
deals with the extent to which the current array of academic programs is
appropriate to the institution's mission. Public governing bodies should
be especially proactive on this question if an institution appears to be
"drifting" away from its assigned role and scope—by offering doctoral
programs at the expense of undergraduate teaching, for example, or by
duplicating the offerings of another nearby publicly funded institution.

This question is not asked as often at private institutions (nor is it
safe to assume that it routinely is asked at publics, either). As always,
exactly how such topics are discussed in boardrooms is a delicate matter often because boards stray from strategic questions towards debates
about content that are properly faculty territory. This means above all
that such discussions should concentrate on the overall *configuration*
of the institution's program offerings—its "center of gravity"—and not
focus unduly on the details of particular academic programs. For example, to generate revenue, quite a few private colleges with an original
liberal arts mission are now offering professional graduate programs.
This is a rational strategy as far as it goes. But the board needs to
ensure that the strategy is deliberate and considered, lest the institution
drift toward a character that was neither planned nor consistent with
its mission and purpose. The board is uniquely positioned to keep such
strategic questions at the forefront of presidential attention.

What's more, academic leaders should be able to identify the *role*
of specific academic programs in the institution's overall array, as well
as the criteria that allow leaders to assess whether the programs are
filling these roles effectively. One scholar of program review, George

Keller, has observed that the best way for board members to look at an institution's array of academic programs as a whole is to consider them as analogous to a portfolio of investments. In a well-balanced investment portfolio, some securities are intended to be held for the long term and are relatively low-risk and low-yield, while others may be intended to secure short-term gains and yield higher dividends at a somewhat greater risk. A small portion of the portfolio may be in the form of secure assets such as gold as an ultimate hedge against downside risk.

When academic programs are viewed as part of an institutional "program portfolio," there are at least three key attributes to consider about each, and academic affairs committees may be particularly interested in applying them in their discussions about particular programs with academic and faculty leaders:

- **Mission Centrality.** The key question here is the extent to which the program "belongs" at the institution regardless of whether it is large or productive. Is it possible to imagine the institution without it? For example, it would be difficult to imagine MIT without a program in computer science or a faith-based college without a major in religious studies.

- **Productivity.** This characteristic is about the efficiency of the program in relation to its cost. Some highly productive programs, regardless of their content, are helpful to the institution because the "profits" they generate can help subsidize the operations of less productive programs that are highly mission-central. On the other hand, institutions probably do not want to have the entire "portfolio" of programs in this category if they lack other desirable characteristics.

- **Quality.** Academic quality is important to monitor because doing so helps identify particular areas of strength in the institution's program portfolio, as well as places where further investment may be beneficial. While all programs should be above a particular threshold of quality, it is always a myth that programs are of "equal" quality with respect to assessed outcomes, faculty background and teaching/research practice, and a host of other factors. Institutional reputations frequently are built on a few academic programs of especially high quality that may be worth subsidizing even though they are not highly productive.

Institutions with the majority of their programs in a favorable position on all three of these characteristics are fortunate indeed, and the art of academic management is to constantly seek improvement in all three, while appropriately balancing the overall "portfolio." Academic leaders should be conscious about these choices and be able to explain them in discussions about academic program quality when this topic comes up in discussions with the academic affairs committee. All board members should be aware of them whenever major investments in new academic directions or program termination is under consideration. If what is regarded as a highly mission-central program is about to be closed because it is unproductive or because quality thresholds have fallen, the right decision may be to reallocate resources from more productive but less mission-central programs to bring productivity and quality back into line. Similarly, if productive programs that are not related to mission are about to be expanded simply to help the bottom line, boards should raise questions about whether such actions will affect mission-related programs or stakeholders' overall perceptions of academic quality. These are long-term strategic questions that sometimes only boards may perceive as important and that board members have a specific responsibility to pose.

2. ***How are we managing program costs?*** Two basic statistics are important in understanding instructional costs at any institution: the proportion of overall expenditures devoted to instruction and instructional costs per student. Roughly speaking, between one-third and two-fifths of every college or university's expenditures goes to support instruction, after deducting research and public-service costs, which vary by institutional type. This proportion may seem surprisingly low to many board members when they first hear it, but it makes sense after one remembers the many things needed to keep an institution operating. These include administrative costs, the operations and maintenance of a large and complex physical plant, and student support services. But because instruction is the only business that every college and university has in common, boards should especially monitor the proportion of resources the institution spends on instruction. Indeed, this matter is important enough that some boards have established policies specifying the minimum proportion of the institution's resources to be spent on instructional functions and include this statistic in their annual set of dashboard indicators.

If the percentage of total expenditures an institution dedicates to instruction provides a measure of its *effort* devoted to instruction, costs per student lets administrators monitor the *efficiency* of this effort. Most institutions calculate this statistic on the basis of full-time-equivalent (FTE) students, though the underlying concept is based on costs per credit hour. Instructional costs often will vary across academic programs—and across apparently similar institutions as well—so boards should understand some of the reasons that drive these differences.

Although some programs will require unusually high investments in equipment or technology, the principal ingredient of instructional costs is the salaries of those who do the teaching in relation to the number of students taught. If a given program is staffed by relatively senior tenured faculty, it naturally will exhibit higher costs than others, just as programs that employ many part-time staff typically will enjoy lower unit costs. Similarly, if the same program suddenly undergoes a significant increase in class size, its instructional costs will decrease. Faculty deployment decisions thus will affect costs to some extent, but much of the institution's instructional cost structure will be relatively immutable because it reflects the seniority and composition of a fixed array of faculty and a fairly established pattern of historical course enrollments.

Academic affairs committees may look at such cost figures as part of their wider engagement with program review. In examining these data, committee members should be careful not to jump to conclusions about high-cost and low-cost programs without asking academic administrators to explain differences in fixed assets and structure. Only after these basic questions have been raised and satisfactorily answered is the committee in a position to discuss with academic leaders what the resulting patterns of expenditure and efficiency imply about academic priorities for investment.

Committee members also should know that these statistics usually are most meaningful when seen in comparative terms. As a result, many colleges and universities monitor instructional expenditure proportions and instructional costs per student against a set of peer institutions that are similar in size, student characteristics, and program mix. For public institutions, moreover, this frequently is done under the auspices of a system office or state coordinating board. Most peer groups of this kind are established to compare faculty salaries and tuition rates—both matters of direct concern that involve decisions typically approved by the board. But they may be useful for other kinds of statistical cost comparisons as well. Consequently, committee members should ask whether such detailed comparisons exist and what institutional leaders think they show.

If such comparisons reveal that the institution's instructional costs are unusually high, committee members should further inquire why administrators think this is happening and whether anything might be done to reduce costs without sacrificing quality. In this regard, all board members should be aware that despite common perceptions that cost and quality go together, some approaches allow savings in instructional cost *without* noticeable declines in learning outcomes. Among these are the following:

- ***Targeting a few high-cost programs for restructuring to improve curricular coherence and substituting lower cost for higher cost faculty in low-enrollment classes.*** This may suggest using peer-group data on instructional costs by department or discipline to identify which programs are targeted and why their costs are out of line in comparison with others.

- ***Reducing the number of low-demand upper division courses offered each term.*** As noted earlier, a significant feature of the instructional landscape in higher education is that faculty members are relatively free to decide what and when they teach. This is a good thing up to a point, but institutions sometimes can realize substantial savings in instructional costs with no difference in ultimate outcomes simply by trimming the undersubscribed courses offered each term that students do not need to complete their programs.

- *Using technology and a redesigned instructional approach in high-enrollment introductory courses.* Every institution has a relatively small number of courses that generate a disproportionate share of its teaching volume. Usually, these are introductory courses such as English composition or introductory psychology that are required for all students or by many majors. These courses are good candidates for redesign because any change in marginal cost per student will be magnified substantially. There can be substantial payoffs from using technology to supplement teaching in areas where it is appropriate—such as communicating content or providing students a way to drill or practice their skills—and using peer tutors to displace high-cost faculty in areas where the latter really are not needed. A recently completed national demonstration project at 30 institutions using such approaches, for instance, demonstrated cost savings of 20 percent to 84 percent with no diminution of learning outcomes, according to the National Center for Academic Transformation.

   Such strategies can appropriately be raised with academic leaders in the academic affairs committee's ongoing dialogue about academic costs and quality. In discussing these matters, though, it again is important to stress that running the instructional program is the job of the faculty and academic leaders, not the board. It is both inappropriate and wasteful for boards on their own to try to identify specific ways to save instructional costs. But board and committee members should be familiar with the basic tools that academic administrators have at their disposal to manage instructional costs, and their minds should not be clouded by an unquestioned assumption that cost and quality are inextricably linked. Instead, they should be prepared to question such assumptions when they are expressed by faculty and academic administrators and inquire whether staff have researched available good practices to contain costs without sacrificing quality.

3. *What counts as program quality?* Chapter 2 offered some detail on the most important view of "quality"—the achievement of desired learning outcomes. But faculty, academic leaders, and external stakeholders may use additional lenses to look at program quality, as well as additional sources of evidence to determine its presence. While maintaining a primary focus on learning outcomes, board members—and especially the members of the academic affairs committee—should consistently question those responsible for academic programs about how *they* define quality and what they are doing to maintain and improve it. Among the many answers supplied may be the following:

- **Reputation.** Although this frequently is denigrated as a factor, what "customers" and peer faculty at other institutions think of a program may be important in helping an institution garner the best students and external resources such as grants or contracts. "Customers" may include students, faculty of graduate programs at other institutions, or employers. The views of peer faculty in the discipline may be especially important because a program's reputation in the field often determines how attractive it will be in hiring the best new faculty. But reputation also is an elusive quality, and it should not necessarily be taken at face value. Additional, more concrete, factors may lie behind a particular program's reputation, and faculty should be able to explain these reasons when asked.

- **Admissions demand.** A straightforward but important mark of success is the program's ability to attract high-quality students. Many institutions ask their entering students what they would like to major in, and this can be compared with the actual numbers of students who end up doing so. In selective institutions, factors such as average SAT or ACT scores and high school ranks and GPAs can be examined across programs. Every faculty wants well-prepared students, so getting them is frequently viewed as a particular earmark of quality.

- **Student satisfaction with their experience in their major.** Studies of undergraduate students repeatedly emphasize the importance of their experience in the major. At most institutions, this experience is determined not only by disciplinary content but also by a range of intangible cultural factors. Some departments are convivial and social, and characterized by unusual levels of student-faculty contact. Some tend to emphasize creating opportunities for "cognitive apprenticeships" such as working with faculty in a research team. Some are especially known for community service or hands-on field work. Student perceptions of the quality of this experience frequently are important factors in a program's reputation.

- **Distinctive curricular features.** It is not surprising that major programs differ substantially in their design across disciplines, but a good deal of curricular variation also may occur across institutions within the same discipline. Frequently, this is because a program has created curricular features that set it apart. Examples may include capstone courses, a common introductory experience, substantial fieldwork or independent work, or a scholarly thesis. The existence of these features may play a big role in the program's attractiveness and in its overall reputation among faculty peers.

- **Employer or graduate demand.** For programs with a vocational or professional focus, employer demand for graduates is an important metric of quality. Are graduates quickly hired? In what types of enterprises do graduates tend to work? Frequently, faculty in such programs pride themselves on less tangible characteristics than employers—for example, that their graduates are "adaptable" or "hands on." Similar feedback may be obtained from faculty at graduate programs to which the program sends students.

- ***Ability to attract external recognition or resources.*** At institutions with a strong research emphasis, a department's reputation is heavily influenced by its ability to attract external grant support. It is not surprising that a similar phenomenon occurs for undergraduate teaching programs. Have they been recognized as outstanding by their disciplinary associations? Have they participated in funded projects or received grants associated with innovations in teaching or curriculum design? Do faculty members earn recognition through institutional or extra-institutional teaching awards?

    How faculty and academic leaders define and recognize program quality is an important factor in their drive to improve it, and academic affairs committee members should listen carefully to what they say. The most important reason is to ensure that discussions about quality improvement are grounded and active, but it also is important to be certain that local definitions of quality are consistent with the institution's overall mission and values. As with more general questions of program mix, there will be a natural tendency for faculty in handling such questions to want to heighten disciplinary recognition and student selectivity as the most important marks of quality. This is expected and for the most part healthy. But committee members need to be sure that all this takes place within the appropriate bounds of mission. If there are signs that such disconnects between mission and programming are becoming serious, the committee should alert the full board for follow-up with the president.

4. ***Who reviews general education?*** By its very nature, program review tends to look at the institution's academic offerings one at a time and in isolation. But some of the most important outcomes of postsecondary education—and many of the aspects that define the distinctiveness of a particular institution—are about more generic attributes of college graduates. As noted in Chapter 2, employers and other external stakeholders especially value such abilities as communication, problem solving, and assuming appropriate responsibility. Board members—and especially members of the academic affairs committee—may be in a unique position to look at program results more holistically and synergistically, and from a perspective that transcends those of individual academic disciplines.

    In this respect, the academic affairs committee may be especially interested in the functioning and effectiveness of the institution's general education program. At most institutions, this will constitute about a third of the undergraduate curriculum and will occur primarily within the first two years of study. Committee members should be aware that because discipline-based departments constitute the heart of academic organization, general education programming has fairly weak administrative and leadership support at most colleges and universities. Most department chairs will think first about staffing graduate courses and courses related to the major, and faculty members within the department will for the most part thank them for it. And though some institutions have explicitly located responsibility for general education in an office reporting to the chief academic officer, they almost always lack a faculty or resources of their own. As a result, responsibility for assuring the quality of general education is dispersed and frequently ineffective.

Program review of a general education program occurs in several ways. Sometimes the review of a department's "service" courses is made an integral part of the regular review. In such cases, academic affairs committee members should ask about what the review says about the quality and the relevance of the department's contribution to this important curricular component if this topic is not explicitly addressed. Occasionally, the institution's general education program is made an independent topic of program review, using the same kinds of guidelines applied to other academic programs. In these cases, committee members should ensure that the results of the review have strong administrative backing and will be given the resources needed to implement any recommendations. Most frequently, however, general education simply is not addressed. Under these circumstances, committee members should explicitly raise the question of who is responsible for assessing and ensuring the quality of general education. If answers are unclear, the matter needs the attention of the chief academic officer and the president.

In discharging responsibility for assuring that the quality of the general education program is carefully examined, board members steer a difficult line. Here, as elsewhere, the faculty has responsibility for academic content, and boards ought to stay out of the way. However, it is arguable that general education is where academic programming is closest to institutional mission, especially for liberal arts or faith-based institutions. Every institution's mission statement has something to say about what all of its graduates have in common and how they will contribute to life and society. In the final analysis, it is up to the board to ensure that these statements are meaningful.

5. *How does program review drive program improvement?*
Because the primary purpose of program review is to improve curriculum and pedagogy, boards should be interested in how this occurs. Some board members, through their service on the academic affairs committee, may have participated directly with faculty and academic leaders in discussing review results. At many institutions, unfortunately,

program review has become ritualized to the point that the information it generates rarely is recognized or used. Sometimes this is because program review is a mandated process. In public institutions where it is required by state authorities but not actively championed or supported by local academic leaders, this may especially be the case. Regardless, academic leaders should take advantage of opportunities to look at program effectiveness, or else the resources invested in them are wasted. Boards have a legitimate interest in seeing that this does not happen.

It is worth noting that connections between review processes and program improvements sometimes may be difficult to detect. Board and committee members should recognize that not all program review results in visible change. Indeed, it has become common for institutional program review or assessment processes to be deemed "ineffective" because nobody *changed* anything. Much of the benefit of a review happens inside the program itself in the form of changes in faculty decisions and behaviors that are not reported to anybody else. A truly reflective faculty will carefully consider what the review has taught them, make the needed changes, and move on. They will request no new resources to implement these improvements, and there will be no written record. It also may be the case that available evidence shows that things are going just fine and that no explicit changes are needed. Informed ratification that sufficient quality is evident is far superior to simply claiming this outcome without really looking.

More subtly, benefits may result in the *way* established things are done, not just in doing new things. Many of the benefits of processes such as program review are cultural in this sense, and they may not be easy to see on the surface. Above all, boards should recognize that a beneficial review process is one in which faculty are willing to visibly and sincerely invest their own time. They will cease to do so if it has no results for them. The academic affairs committee, therefore, should explore with academic administrators specifically whether these more subtle forms of improvement have occurred.

All board members also should be aware of any formal connections between program review and established institutional decision processes. Are program review results considered in the institutional planning process, and if so, what kinds of results can be traced? For instance, some institutions have discovered that particular themes repeatedly occur across programs after looking at the results of reviews alongside one another. Many programs may be encountering similar challenges in harnessing instructional technology, for example, or in implementing experiential learning approaches or pedagogies that emphasize active learning. These have clear collective implications for faculty development that ought to be pursued. Do program review results have budgetary implications and, if so, of what typical kinds?

Many critics of program review simply see it as a channel for departments to ask for new resources, but it is fair for boards to use it to ask for evidence. If departmental requests for new resources that are supported by good evidence are treated in the same way in the budgetary processes as departmental requests that are not, it is clear that the results of program review are not connected to decisions that matter. Once again, sensitivity in inquiring about these matters is essential: It is not the board's prerogative to second-guess individual budgetary decisions. But if the responses of academic leaders suggest that assessment and review processes are not connected to decision making (a condition, experience suggests, into which colleges and universities unconsciously may drift), the board needs to remind academic leaders of their responsibility.

The board should ensure that all four of the foregoing processes are working together as part of a larger institutional approach to planning and decision making. Too often, processes such as assessment, managing retention, looking at student and stakeholder opinion, and program review are pursued as independent activities by different actors with different motivations and intentions. Apart from the president, board members are among the few individuals who can determine whether these processes are connected to one another to systematically inform investments and strategic decisions. If there are doubts about whether this is occurring often enough, board members have an obligation to raise the issue with the president and to insist that the matter be addressed. Integration is something that boards clearly understand and act upon in the realm of fiscal affairs where revenue generation, resource allocation, and fiscal accountability must all work together to ensure responsible budgeting and financial management. It ought to be equally understood and acted upon by boards when they discharge their responsibility for academic affairs.

# CHAPTER 6

# Accreditation: The Quality Test

The topic of institutional and program accreditation returns our discussion of the board's role in academic quality assurance to the notion of fiduciary responsibility. Accreditation is the established "quality test" for the academy. It performs much the same role for the institution's academic operations as a financial audit does for its fiscal affairs. This parallel is worth delineating along several dimensions.

First, like a clean audit, a favorable accreditation decision provides a clear public signal to stakeholders and potential customers that the institution and its academic programs operate with integrity and have attained a recognized level of performance that can be relied upon. Like a financial audit, a clean bill of health is the expected and usual outcome. But negative findings, though they occur infrequently, can spell real trouble. Loss of accreditation means loss of funding through participation in federal student financial-aid programs and sends a strong market message to potential students that the institution either is untrustworthy or its programs are of inferior quality. The board needs to ensure that the administration does not allow this to happen.

Second, like a financial audit, the principal focus of accreditation is on the institution's own *processes* for ensuring academic quality and integrity. A financial audit in essence certifies through external review that the institution conducts its fiscal business according to "generally accepted accounting procedures" and that, therefore, its fiscal statements and claims about its bottom line can be trusted. Accreditation, in essence, performs the same function regarding claims about academic quality—especially with respect to the achievement of acceptable student-learning outcomes.

Accreditors will rarely make explicit statements about the overall quality of student learning exhibited by the institution's graduates. Rather, by examining how colleges and universities *verify* their *own* claims about learning, they assess the level of confidence and trust that external observers should place on these claims.

Third, as with a financial audit, results of an accreditation encounter are of two kinds. A public declaration of the institution's accredited status is the visible component—a straightforward determination of where the institution stands that is similar to the contents of a financial audit report. But some of the most valuable information that results from accreditation lies in the confidential team report and "action letter" that accompanies the public declaration of accredited status. Like the "management letter" that accompanies a financial audit, this document advises the institution privately about matters of concern to which it ought to attend promptly to avoid future difficulties with accredited status. Accreditation action letters can address a range of topics, but some of the most important will focus on improvements that should be made in academic quality-assurance processes. Boards should pay particular attention to these to be sure they understand what accreditors are saying and that academic leaders are addressing these issues.

Most important, like the inevitable review of financial procedures that results from an audit, an accreditation visit is an opportunity for the institution to learn. Far too many presidents and program directors see accreditation fundamentally as a burden—something that periodically must be endured to maintain a "Good Housekeeping seal of approval," but that represents a diversion of resources away from core functions. Adopting such a compliance-only mentality is a mistake for two reasons. First, such apathy often is picked up by accreditors themselves who look for genuine engagement in the review process as an important marker of a "quality culture." More important, a half-hearted approach to accreditation means wasting resources on something that "adds no value." If accreditation is a required activity that entails institutional costs, and if the process really can be harnessed by the faculty and academic leaders to reveal solid information about how academic programs are functioning and how they can be improved, then clearly the institution should take full advantage. Fortunately, accrediting organizations increasingly are structuring their reviews to allow institutions to do so. Boards should know this and should be prepared to ask institutional leaders about these possibilities and how the institution can take advantage of them.

## The Basics.

Accreditation comes in two flavors—institutional and programmatic—and while both are important, they differ in focus and consequences.

- Institutional accreditation is a uniquely American approach to quality assurance that began as a voluntary review process about a century ago, when individual colleges and universities needed a mechanism to accept one another's degrees and credits. It currently is governed through eight separate, independent regional commissions that are membership organizations comprising the institutions they accredit.

- Programmatic accreditation, or specialized accreditation, looks at individual academic offerings in occupational or professional fields, usually under the auspices of an accrediting commission established by a professional association that governs the conduct of the profession as a whole.

Institutional accreditation is centered in and owned by the academy, while programmatic accreditation usually is not.

The review process undertaken by both institutional and programmatic accrediting organizations typically involves three steps: (1) a comprehensive self-study prepared by the institution or program according to guidelines provided by the accreditor; (2) a multiday visit by an accreditation team of peer reviewers comprising faculty and administrators who prepare a report to the accrediting commission that examines the institution or program against standards established by the commission; and (3) a commission action that either continues the institution or program's accreditation and/or imposes sanctions and offers recommendations.

The established institutional accreditation cycle is ten years, while programmatic accreditation cycles tend to be about three to five years. But there has been a general trend among all accreditors to ask about progress in meeting recommendations and/or to undertake limited site visits "off cycle" to look at particular issues. Except for the accreditation decision itself, the process typically is confidential, and most accrediting organizations consciously construct their engagement with institutions as consultative, not as an agent of accountability.

Institutional accreditation's interest in "quality" has always been comprehensive—embracing matters ranging from the adequacy of resources, the appropriateness of institutional governance arrangements, faculty qualifications, and adequate providing of instruction. This interest has been pursued for more than a century and continues to be important for visiting teams today. But with the Higher Education Act (HEA) of 1965, institutional accreditation was assigned a new high-stakes role by the federal government as the "gatekeeper" for institutional eligibility to participate in such federal financial-aid programs as Pell Grants and guaranteed student loans.

Through the HEA, Congress has tasked institutional accreditors with determining the answers to two questions on behalf of the federal government: (1) Does each institution have the fiscal and organizational infrastructure in place to ensure that it can serve as a trustworthy steward of federal funds? (2) Are the institution's academic offerings of sufficient quality that students will benefit from them (and be in a position to pay off their loans)? Since they assumed this "gatekeeping" role, institutional accreditors increasingly have been asked to review matters related to the second question—including, most prominently in recent years, the quality of student-learning outcomes.

Programmatic accreditation, by contrast, always has been more narrowly focused. Certainly programmatic accreditors are interested in the basic institutional infrastructure within which programs operate. But they are far more interested in whether the program they are looking at is adequately supported by the institution with respect to resources and is given a fairly free hand in how it operates and governs itself.

These two interests mean that presidents sometimes are ambivalent about the process. On the one hand, achieving accredited status in a professional program such as business or engineering may enhance the program's marketability and therefore its ability to generate revenue. On the other hand, the program's leaders often will use the "need to maintain accreditation" as leverage for requesting increasingly more resources and operating independence at the expense of the institution as a whole. Boards, as "keepers of the mission," need to understand these dynamics because it is easy for institutions to be overly concerned with satisfying the narrowly conceived interests of programs that can mobilize this kind of leverage. And they should recognize that institutional accreditation is something the institution cannot do without, while the decision to seek or maintain programmatic accreditation is essentially a management issue centered on marketing and program-investment priorities.

Boards also should be aware that accreditation practice is changing, and for the most part, these changes can benefit institutions. Many institutional accreditors are trying to visibly distinguish their "compliance" role from their role in providing institutional consultation and improvement. The primary force behind this change was pressure from institutions whose basic accreditation status was not at risk; these schools had grown weary of what appeared to be costly and ritualistic reviews that added little to campus planning and management processes. The result, for virtually all of institutional accreditation, is a far more flexible review approach that gives institutions unprecedented opportunity to use the accreditation process to engage a set of quality issues of their own choosing. This will happen only to if presidents are aware of these opportunities and decide to act on them. Boards should make sure that such opportunities, if they are present, are appropriately recognized.

Finally, boards should be aware that institutional accreditation standards frequently require their own participation in the accreditation process and that the effectiveness of the institution's governance arrangements—including the scope and delivery of board oversight—will be part of what is examined. As a result, board members should be familiar with the standards addressing governance established by their institutional accreditor and the specific roles boards are expected to play (and not play) in institutional and academic governance.

Well in advance of a visit, board members should review past accreditation results and know that trustees are expected to be broadly aware of the administration's plans to address any recommendations that result from a review. Most accreditation visits also will feature meetings with the board chair and/or selected board members to discuss how the board functions in its oversight role. Board members should expect these meetings to include questions about the board's awareness of the institution's key academic quality-assurance processes, and board members should be prepared for such questions if they arise.

# Questions for Boards to Consider.

At the most basic level, boards should be broadly aware of the institution's accreditation status, the institution's current place in the accreditation cycle, and the most important issues that arose during its last accreditation visit. Board attention to programmatic accreditation is appropriately less salient, but the board should know which programs at the institution are accredited by such organizations, and it should be aware of plans to seek accreditation in others if this is an emerging goal. Beyond these basics, the following questions related to accreditation may be useful for boards to pursue:

1.  ***What progress have we made in addressing recommendations from the last review?*** One frequently voiced reservation about institutional accreditation is that it operates on a very long cycle. Although many institutional accreditors contact colleges and universities more frequently than once every ten years, this usually involves something like a five-year interim report or a focused visit to follow up on a specific concern. As a result, there is some tendency for faculty and staff to heave a collective sigh of relief after reaffirmation occurs and not think much about what needs to be done until it is time to gear up for the next review.

    The recommendations that usually emerge from an institutional review tend to be systemic, raising such issues as administrative infrastructure and communication, governance, diversity, or strategic planning—issues that often take some time to address. As a result, it is prudent for boards periodically to ask the institution's leadership for an update on outstanding concerns that arose from the last accreditation review, about what is being done to address these concerns, and what progress has been made. This need not be a lengthy activity, but it ought to occur annually on a regular schedule.

    From a larger perspective, institution leaders need to acknowledge that when they complete an accreditation cycle, they probably know more about the institution than ever. Typically, institutional self-studies have compiled, organized, and examined enormous bodies of data about finance, enrollment trends, instructional resources, and program assets that seldom are examined in such a comprehensive fashion. Similarly, most institutions use the occasion of accreditation to conduct a range of additional studies such as student and stakeholder surveys, alumni or employer studies, or special assessments of student learning. Because of its size and scope, this level of evidence gathering and analysis is impossible to maintain indefinitely. But it ought not disappear entirely.

    Unfortunately, many institutions allow the planning and evaluation assets built through self-study to atrophy once the current accreditation cycle ends. This means that this extensive (and expensive) apparatus must be reconstructed from scratch when the next accreditation cycle comes around. Not only is this wasteful, it also prevents continuity in the evidence that may be examined over time—for example, posing a few of the same questions to alumni in the same way so that trends can be established. One of the virtues of newer alternative accreditation approaches is that they emphasize doing fewer things with respect to evidence and analysis, but doing them more consistently over time.

Boards should be aware of this common institutional dynamic and at the conclusion of an accreditation encounter be prepared to ask institutional leaders how they plan to sustain the momentum for planning and evaluation generated by the impetus of accreditation. Several mechanisms exist to accomplish this. Campus leaders should be asked to review the results of an institutional accreditation review with the board soon after its conclusion and to discuss explicit plans for addressing its recommendations. One part of this review might include determining which bodies of evidence to maintain over time for strategic planning purposes and to help prepare for the next accreditation visit. Briefly reviewing progress on these plans each year with the board might be made a regular expectation. Similar provisions addressing accreditation might be included in the board's annual review of presidential performance and be established as expectations for new presidents.

This last point may be especially important in the light of decreasing average presidential tenures, which at about six years are well within the typical ten-year accreditation cycle. A board opportunity for raising this issue may arise when boards ensure that brief updates on progress to address recommendations of the last accreditation review are built into the board's annual calendar. New presidents should be reminded early in their tenure (or even as part of the search process) of past commitments to maintain strategic planning assets made by their predecessors. They also should be asked how they intend to discharge or modify these plans.

2. *What progress have we made in assessing student-learning outcomes?* Regardless of whether the topic of assessing student-learning outcomes was explicitly cited by an accreditation review team—and it usually is these days—boards should pay special attention to ensuring that the topic continues to be addressed. Accrediting organizations will continue to move strongly in the direction of making the institution's processes for assessing student learning the centerpiece of their examination of academic quality assurance.

To reiterate the argument of Chapter 2, they will expect every academic program to have visible statements of learning outcomes, collect credible evidence that these outcomes are being achieved, and demonstrate how the resulting information is being used to improve teaching and learning. They will have the same expectation for general education and other cross-cutting curricular requirements. Knowing that assessment practice is still relatively new in higher education, accreditors have given institutions time to put these mechanisms into place, and up to now they have been relatively lenient in enforcing their assessment standards. But because the federal government increasingly is holding accreditors themselves accountable, this situation cannot be maintained indefinitely. Boards should be fully advised that continuing inattention to assessment involves risk to their institutions.

Board members also should be aware of the many persistent myths about what accreditors "really want" with respect to learning assessment. One of these myths is that only standardized tests are credible to accreditors as evidence of student learning. Institutions and programs frequently assume that examinations of this kind will satisfy review teams because of their perceived rigor and public credibility. And such measures may well be appropriate to particular kinds of learning and in particular programmatic contexts. But accreditors actually are seeking instances where faculty have chosen assessment approaches that match the types of learning being emphasized and whose results are usable and used.

Similar myths surround the use of qualitative assessment approaches or those based on expert and peer judgments of student performance. Despite prevalent rhetoric, "measurable" outcomes are not always what accreditors are looking for. But perceptions *are* correct that external reviewers are seeking direct evidence of student academic achievement, so assessment programs based solely on student satisfaction surveys will likely receive negative comments from a visiting team.

3. ***Are our accreditable programs accredited?*** Programmatic accreditation can be a mixed blessing for colleges and universities. On the one hand, the external recognition provided by accreditation can enhance a program's reputation and marketability. These are substantial advantages, and if the programs are accreditable by a recognized professional body, they always will benefit from achieving accredited status. But is this good for the institution? Programmatic accreditation sometimes carries with it a substantial price tag with respect to direct costs and the organizational "overhead" associated with responding to a large and diverse array of external review bodies. At a large university, for example, it is not unusual for there to be three or four visits from programmatic accreditors underway each year.

More subtly, maintaining accreditation may require the institution to invest scarce resources in things that may not be consistent with established mission or planning priorities. For example, accreditation standards in some fields may mandate a particular student-faculty ratio, require faculty to engage in a specified amount of recognized research, or call for investments in special facilities that are inconsistent with what the institution is doing for equally important but non-accreditable academic programs. These are important trade-offs, and board members should be aware of them.

Members of the academic affairs committee may play a more explicit role in advising on the strategic choices involved in seeking or maintaining specialized accreditation. Members should know which of the institution's programs are in fact accredited by a professional body as well as those that could be but are not. In some cases—in most programs in health-related fields, for example—programmatic accreditation essentially is required: Individuals must be graduates of an accredited program in order to practice. But in other prominent professional fields, business or engineering, for example, accredited status is not required. In still others, teacher education, for example, requirements for accredited status vary by state. And in fields such as business, teacher education, and nursing, there may be several programmatic accreditors to choose from when seeking recognition.

Under these conditions, the decision to seek or maintain programmatic accreditation is complex and needs to be understood on a case-by-case basis. But it is important for academic affairs committee members to recognize that with the exception of those few programs where accreditation is a requirement, this is a *business* decision that should ride on weighing the associated costs and benefits. Academic affairs committees may provide presidents and academic leaders with useful advice on how to approach this decision from a disinterested standpoint—"above the fray" of academic politics. Above all, when they provide such advice, board members should do so from the point of view of their prime role as "keepers of the institution's mission."

4. ***What do we hope to learn from our engagement with accreditation?*** Institutional and programmatic accreditation represents a considerable and, to some people, surprising investment of institutional resources. A medium-size college or university routinely devotes the equivalent of two full-time administrative staff positions and must allow substantial faculty release time to the process during the two years or so it is preparing for institutional reaffirmation. The direct costs of the process easily can total six figures. This is, of course, a necessary price to pay for remaining in good standing with the federal government and the academic community, and it probably represents a good marketing investment as well.

Again, institutions are not getting their money's worth from the process of self-examination that accreditation provides if they treat it simply as a routine compliance exercise. One of the most important questions board members should ask when the time for institutional reaccreditation rolls around, therefore, is how the administration plans to use accreditation as an opportunity to learn and improve.

Virtually all of the regional commissions that accredit institutions have changed their review processes in the past few years to allow institutions greater flexibility to address topics of their own choosing. In some cases, this is built into the process—for example, in the Educational Effectiveness review required by the Western Association Senior Commission, the Quality Enhancement Plan required by the Southern Association, or the processes selected for continuous review and improvement under the Higher Learning Commission's AQIP approach based on the Malcolm Baldrige National Quality Award. Boards of institutions operating under these auspices should know the particular topics the institution has selected for in-depth study and the reasons why these topics were chosen. But boards of institutions located in other accreditation jurisdictions also should know that all of the regions now allow "thematic," "focused," or "special topic" self-studies on a case-by-case basis.

Institutions taking this approach must demonstrate that they meet all established accreditation standards by submitting documents and exhibits that show compliance. Instead of writing a traditional descriptive self-study narrative that systematically addresses each accreditation standard, they prepare an analytical document that examines in depth two or three topics that have been approved by the accreditation commission. Examples might include the effectiveness of the undergraduate first-year experience program, improving retention and success among students of color, or creating a more student-centered learning environment.

Accreditors, however, expect most of the topics to be related to the core task of undergraduate education in the realm of teaching and learning. Academic affairs committees may be especially helpful in providing academic leaders with advice about which topics to choose because they are focused primarily on the strategic questions the institution needs to answer about its academic programs. They also may be in a good position to assess which potential topics are the most symbolically powerful in demonstrating the institution's strengths and distinctiveness to outside stakeholders.

Accrediting organizations also are increasingly interested in looking at an institution's capacity for self-evaluation and improvement, and this emphasis is reflected in their standards. Instead of inspecting this capacity directly by looking at processes such as assessment, institutional research, and program review, the topical self-study approach allows accreditors an opportunity to view the institution's evaluation assets "in motion" as they are applied to a particular topic or problem. This gives institutions the chance to demonstrate compliance at the same time they learn something useful about themselves. Because this is an important "win-win" situation, boards should know whether the institution is in a position to take advantage of it.

Board members also should know that there are sometimes good reasons why the institution's leadership may not want to go down this path. These alternative approaches are most applicable and useful for colleges and universities that already are in a fairly strong position with respect to accreditation—that is, if they went through the traditional accreditation process, they would emerge problem-free. Such institutions already have all the needed documentation to quickly fulfill the "compliance" portion of a review in order to get on with its topical component. But many institutions may benefit from the discipline associated with documenting the fact that internal quality-assurance processes such as assessment, course and program approval and review, and faculty promotion and tenure are in place and effective. Adopting a traditional accreditation approach is a good way to get this done.

Furthermore, precisely because these new approaches to institutional review are more flexible and open-ended, they also are more uncertain. Presidents know that when they engage in such reviews they will need to work carefully with the accrediting organization to delineate the scope of the visiting team's inquiry. With fewer guidelines to constrain them, visiting team members sometimes can become "loose cannons," so adopting the safer traditional approach to self-study may be an appropriate choice. For these and other reasons, presidents may elect not to take advantage of some of the newer and more flexible approaches to review that accreditors now offer. Boards should know the reasons for this decision, and wise presidents will seek the board's counsel about it. Even if this more traditional course of action is adopted, the question of how the institution plans to take advantage of the accreditation opportunity as a learning experience, however it is structured, should continue to be posed.

Finally, all board members should remember that academic accreditation is a uniquely American practice that needs their support. In most other countries, responsibility for assuring and maintaining the quality of colleges and universities rests with a government ministry, which typically pays for higher education as well. In the United States, this responsibility is vested collectively in the higher education enterprise itself. The legal and operational independence that results has allowed our higher education system to become the most diverse and entrepreneurial in the world—and, most would still say, the best.

American higher education will be able to maintain this status only if the academy takes seriously its historic role to maintain its own integrity through the self-regulatory process of institutional accreditation. Boards have a clear responsibility to their institutions to ensure that they are operating with integrity and delivering high-quality academic programs. But they have an equally important collective responsibility to the nation to ensure that self-regulation remains a reliable guarantor of academic quality and integrity. This means being aware of the process at their own institutions, and it occasionally may mean asking hard questions. Allowing accreditation to become empty and ritualistic is a sure invitation for excessive government regulation, which likely would be unhealthy for academic vitality. In their collective role of custodians of the academy, boards should be perpetually wary of this possibility and should do their best to keep self-regulation vital.

# Epilogue

I am privileged to serve as a board member at Truman State University in Missouri, an institution that has a long tradition of assessing student learning and making use of the results to improve instruction. And I am proud that this institution has been cited as exemplary on several occasions for its efforts in this arena by its regional accrediting organization. We have had a succession of fine presidents who have kept these matters at the forefront of the institution's agenda. But in my "day job" as a consultant and commentator on higher education accountability and instructional improvement, I am forced to admit that there are far too few presidents or institutions that have made these matters of high priority.

As Derek Bok, distinguished former (and now interim) president of Harvard University, eloquently put it in a December 16, 2005, essay on the board's role in academic affairs in the *Chronicle of Higher Education*:

> *Presidents are the natural source of initiative to see that problems of student learning are identified and reforms are developed. In practice, however, few presidents have made serious, sustained efforts to play that role. Perhaps they fear opposition from their faculty or adverse publicity if they discuss weaknesses in their institutions' educational product. Perhaps they are too busy balancing budgets and raising money. Certainly the easiest course is to direct their energies toward more visible and less controversial goals, such as increasing average SAT scores or building imposing new facilities.*
>
> *Do trustees have a role in overcoming this weakness? Surely not by taking it upon themselves to evaluate the quality of education and to recommend improvements. Such actions would exceed their competence and antagonize the faculty. A better course would be for trustees to ask the president to report on current procedures for assessing the effectiveness of the faculty's teaching and for developing better ways to educate students.*
>
> *Once trustees have received answers to their questions, they can urge the president to work with the faculty to make the college a more effective learning organization and report periodically on the result. By so doing, trustees would not presume to dictate how professors should teach their courses. But trustees would give the quality of education a much higher place among the college's priorities. Presidents would receive a powerful*

*mandate to press ahead with programs of assessment and experimentation rather than succumb to the forces of inertia and indifference that so often stifle such initiatives.... If priorities are to change to put greater emphasis on the quality of education, someone will have to alter the incentives and rewards that currently influence academic leaders. No one but the trustees seems capable of accomplishing that result.*

These are wise, though provocative, words. Achieving the proper balance in advocating for academic quality assurance and improvement will be a perpetual challenge for every board—including my own. But such advocacy is a part of our basic responsibility. It is my fond hope that this book will provide committed board members with a place to start and a few resources to continue this important task.

66

*Epilogue*

# About the Author

Peter T. Ewell is vice president of the National Center for Higher Education Management Systems (NCHEMS) in Boulder, Colo., and a trustee of Truman State University in Missouri. NCHEMS is a research and development center founded to improve the management effectiveness of colleges and universities.

Ewell's work focuses on assessing institutional effectiveness and the outcomes of a college education. He is involved both in research and direct consulting with institutions and state systems on collecting and using assessment information for planning, evaluation, and budgeting. A staff member since 1981, he has directed many projects on assessment, including initiatives funded by the W. K. Kellogg Foundation, the National Institute for Education, the Consortium for the Advancement of Private Higher Education, and the Pew Charitable Trusts. He currently is a principal partner in the Pew Forum on Undergraduate Learning.

In addition, Ewell has consulted with more than 375 colleges and universities and 24 state systems of higher education on such topics as assessment, program review, enrollment management, and student retention. He also has been actively involved in NCHEMS work on longitudinal student databases and other academic management and information tools.

Ewell has written six books and numerous articles about improving undergraduate instruction through the assessment of student outcomes. Among his books are *The Self-Regarding Institution: Information for Excellence* and *Assessing Educational Outcomes*, both of which have been widely cited in the development of campus-based assessment programs. In 1998, he led the design team for the National Survey of Student Engagement (NSSE) and currently chairs its Technical Advisory Panel.

Before joining NCHEMS, Ewell was coordinator for long-range planning at Governors State University. A graduate of Haverford College, he received his Ph.D. in political science from Yale University in 1976 and was on the faculty of the University of Chicago.

# Index

71

*Making The Grade*

**73**

*Making The Grade*